SCIENCE
for FUN
EXPERIMENTS

© Aladdin Books Ltd 1996
Designed and produced by
Aladdin Books Ltd
28 Percy Street
London W1P OLD

First published in the United States by
Copper Beech Books,
an imprint of
The Millbrook Press
2 Old New Milford Road
Brookfield, Connecticut 06804

Design: David West Children's Book Design
Illustrator: Tony Kenyon
Photography: Roger Vlitos
Models: David Millea

**Library of Congress
Cataloging-in-Publication Data**
Gibson, Gary, 1957–
Science for fun experiments / by Gary Gibson; illustrated by Tony Kenyon.
p. cm. Includes index.
Summary: Provides instructions for a selection of hands-on experiments
introducing basic scientific principles,
in such areas as magnetism, electricity, and water.
ISBN 0-7613-0517-3 (pbk.)
1. Science---Experiments---Juvenile
literature. [1. Science--Experiments.
2. Experiments.] I. Kenyon, Tony. Ill. II. Title.
Q164.G524 1996 96-13908
507' .8--dc20 CIP AC

SCIENCE
for FUN

EXPERIMENTS

GARY GIBSON

COPPER BEECH BOOKS
Brookfield, Connecticut

CONTENTS

CHAPTER SIX
Making Things Float and Sink 138-163

INTRODUCTION

Have you ever wondered what would happen to the Earth if there were no sunlight? Have you thought about where magnetism comes from, or what life would be like without electricity?

You will probably have tried to walk as a weightless astronaut, and come down to Earth with a bump and wondered why that happens. But have you wondered why a submarine can both sink and float? Do you understand how musical instruments make sounds?

For centuries scientists have worked to find out more about these things. They have investigated light and color, shapes, pushing and pulling, and why and how things change. They have also experimented with floating and sinking,

electricity, magnetism, and sound.

Science for Fun Experiments introduces you to some of the fascinating discoveries that have been made about these scientific phenomena. It takes you step-by-step through fun, "hands-on" experiments, giving you a brief explanation of why they work, so you can impress you friends with your scientific knowledge! You will learn how to make useful gadgets – a stethoscope, a banger, a compass, a jet boat, a motor, even 3-D glasses – to name just a few of the exciting projects.

Whenever this symbol appears, adult supervision is required.

CONTENTS

CHAPTER *One*

LIGHT AND COLOR

LIGHT FOR LIFE

Green plants need sunlight to live and grow. They use the light's energy to grow. All animals get their food from plants, either directly or indirectly. Since plants need sunlight to grow, all living things depend on the sun.

GROWING WATERCRESS

1 Put a layer of cotton in the bottom of two clean dishes. Add a little water. Sprinkle watercress seeds evenly over the cotton.

2 Put the dishes on a sunny windowsill and cover each dish with a cardboard box. Make a hole in the side of one box and leave for several days. Check daily that the cotton is damp.

3 The seeds under the box with no hole have grown straight up looking for light. The watercress under the box with the hole has grown toward the light.

WHY IT WORKS

Green plants contain a chemical called chlorophyll. Chlorophyll traps light, which combines with water and air to help make plants grow. This process is called "photosynthesis." Plants cannot see light but can bend and grow toward where it comes from.

Sunlight

Air

Water

FURTHER IDEAS

Follow step 1 again. Cover one dish with a large, clean glass jar to make a "greenhouse." Compare the growing roots and shoots with the uncovered dish. Which seedlings grow the best?

DAY AND NIGHT

Half the world is in daylight and the other half in darkness. As the Earth spins around, each part takes its turn to face the sun. Parts of the Earth facing away from the sun can be lit only by the moon. Sometimes the moon passes between the sun and the Earth, so the sun's rays are blocked and the sky grows dark. This is called an eclipse.

MAKE A SUNDIAL

1 You need a piece of wood, or thick cardboard, and a length of dowel. Make a hole near one edge of the wood for the dowel.

2 Stand the dowel in the hole (fix with glue if necessary). Decorate using waterproof paints.

3 On a sunny morning put the sundial outside. The dowel casts a shadow; paint along the shadow.

4 Repeat step 3 every hour. Paint the time next to each shadow. The sundial will only work on sunny days. Remember to keep it in the same place, facing the same way.

WHY IT WORKS

The stick blocks the sun and casts a shadow. The shadow's position changes as the sun moves across the sky.

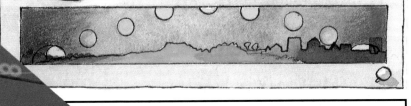

As the Earth spins around, the sun appears to move across the sky.

FURTHER IDEAS
Make a shadow animal with your hands. In a darkened room, get a friend to shine a flashlight onto the wall. Put your hands in front of the flashlight and see if you can make an animal-shaped shadow on the wall.

SEEING IMAGES

An image is a likeness of something or someone. What we see in photographs or a movie are images. A camera is a box that can make an image on photographic film. The film contains chemicals that will keep the image for years.

MAKE A PINHOLE CAMERA

1 Find a small cardboard box that does not let light through. Use a pair of scissors to cut out one side of the box.

2 Tape a piece of tracing paper over the cutout side of the box. Make sure that the tracing paper is kept as smooth as possible.

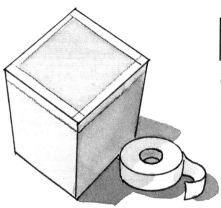

3 Make a pinhole in the side of the box opposite the tracing paper. Point the pinhole at a window. Move toward the window until you see its image on the tracing paper.

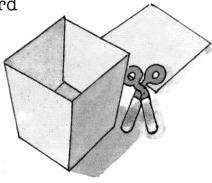

WHY IT WORKS

Light rays in air do not bend or curve; they always travel in straight lines. Rays of light from the window enter the pinhole in straight lines and hit the tracing paper. The light rays from the bottom and the top of the window cross over as they pass through the hole, so the image appears upside down.

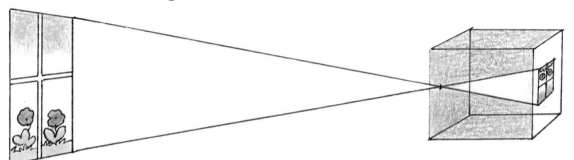

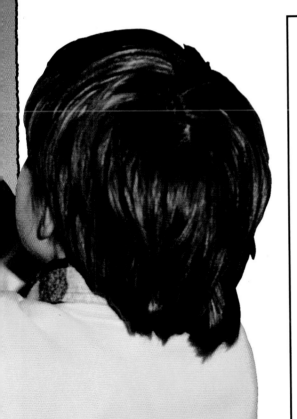

FURTHER IDEAS

Make the pinhole a little bigger so more light enters the camera. The image becomes brighter but less clear. A magnifying glass in front of the pinhole can sharpen the image. The image will be faint, so point the pinhole at a bright object such as a lightbulb.

BOUNCING LIGHT

Rays of light can be bounced off an object like a rubber ball bouncing off a wall. We call this "reflection." Light rays are reflected best by flat, shiny surfaces such as shiny spoons, cans, bottles, or mirrors.

MAKE A KALEIDOSCOPE

1 Carefully tape together three identical-sized small mirrors. Make a triangle-shaped tube with the shiny sides facing inside.

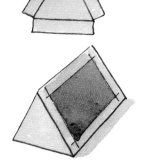

2 Cut out a triangle-shaped piece of paper, allowing for flaps. Tape it over one end of the triangle of mirrors to form a box.

3 Cut out small pieces of brightly colored paper from a magazine and drop them into the bottom of the box.

16

4 Tape another triangle of paper over the other end of the tube. Using a pencil, make a hole to look through. The kaleidoscope is finished.

5 Hold the kaleidoscope level, and point it at a bright light. Look at the pattern through the eye piece. Shake and look again.

WHY IT WORKS

Light rays from the colored paper are reflected back and forth between the mirrors. Each image is doubled by the mirrors before the light rays reach your eye.

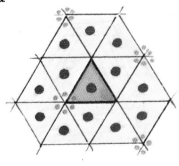

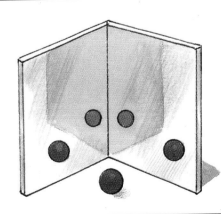

FURTHER IDEAS
Stand two mirrors up at right angles, using modeling clay. Place a marble between the mirrors. How many images can you see?

UP PERISCOPE!

Submarine crews want to know what is going on above the waves without being seen. Instead of rising to the ocean's surface, the submarine raises its periscope. On land you can use periscopes to see over walls and around corners!

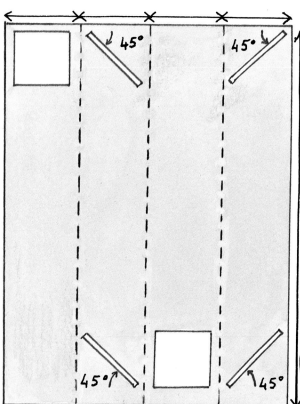

MAKE A PERISCOPE

45° 45°

45° 45°

1 Copy the pattern onto cardboard. Cut around the outline. Cut out the slots and squares. Fold on the dotted lines.

2 Tape the edges of the cardboard together to form a box. Make sure that the slots line up. Paint to decorate.

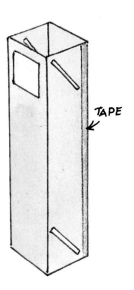

TAPE

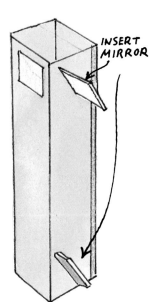

INSERT MIRROR

3 Insert two mirrors into the slots, top mirror facing down, bottom mirror facing up. Look into the lower mirror.

WHY IT WORKS

Light rays above and ahead of you hit the upper mirror. It reflects the rays down to the lower mirror, which in turn reflects the light rays into your eyes.

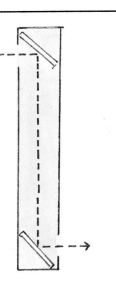

FURTHER IDEAS

Make a periscope to see around corners. Copy the design shown below. Follow instructions 1 and 2 as before. But this time the angles of the mirror slots are different. Make sure the top mirror faces down and the bottom mirror faces up.

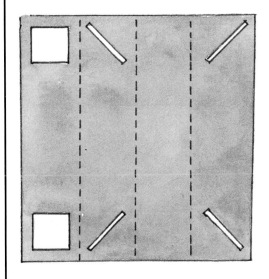

MOVING PICTURES

Cartoon films are made out of many drawings. These are photographed one after another by a movie camera. When the film is projected onto a screen, the images seem to move. If you move your eyes quickly over the pictures on the right, the ball seems to bounce.

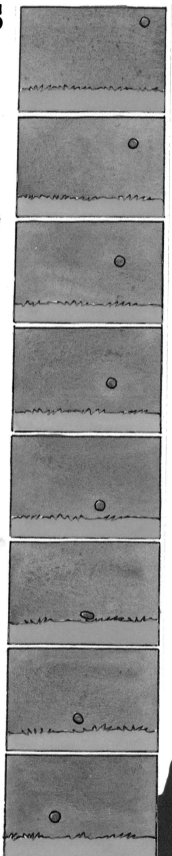

MAKE A FLICK BOOK

1 Draw a background picture. Trace it onto at least 12 pages of the same size. Leave a margin down one side of each drawing.

2 Draw the sun high in the sky on the first page. Draw it slightly lower on the second page. Repeat until the sun has set on the last page.

3 Stack the pages neatly and staple them together with two staples along the edge of the margin.

WHY IT WORKS

Your eyes see each image for a fraction of a second. If the images are shown fast enough, the eye runs the images together. Differences in the separate images appear as movement.

FURTHER IDEAS
Copy the two faces (below) onto two sheets of tracing paper. Staple the two sheets together. Roll the upper sheet tightly around a pencil. Move the pencil up and down to roll and unroll the upper sheet.

4 Hold the flick book by the margin and watch the sun go down as you flick the pages.

SPLITTING LIGHT

More than 300 years ago, Sir Isaac Newton proved that white light is made from the colors of the rainbow. Newton split white light into a rainbow using a wedge of glass called a prism. We see rainbows in the sky because water droplets in the air split the sunlight before it reaches us.

2 Angle a mirror in a bowl of water. Bend a large piece of white posterboard away from the bowl.

MAKE A RAINBOW

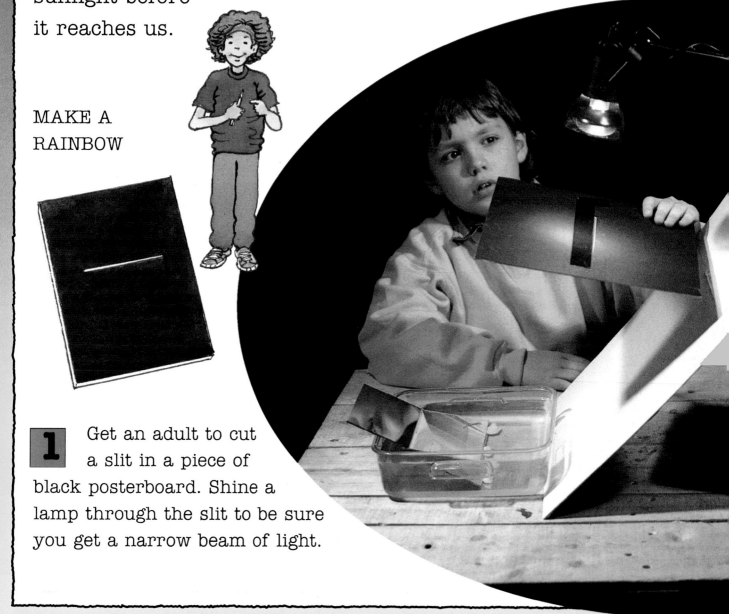

1 Get an adult to cut a slit in a piece of black posterboard. Shine a lamp through the slit to be sure you get a narrow beam of light.

3 Shine a light through the slit in the black posterboard and onto the mirror. Adjust both pieces of posterboard until you get the best rainbow.

4 You should be able to see all seven colors of the rainbow.

WHY IT WORKS

When a beam of light shines into glass or water, it bends. Each of the colors in white light bends at a slightly different angle. This causes the colors to split apart. Each color reflected from the mirror becomes spread out on the screen.

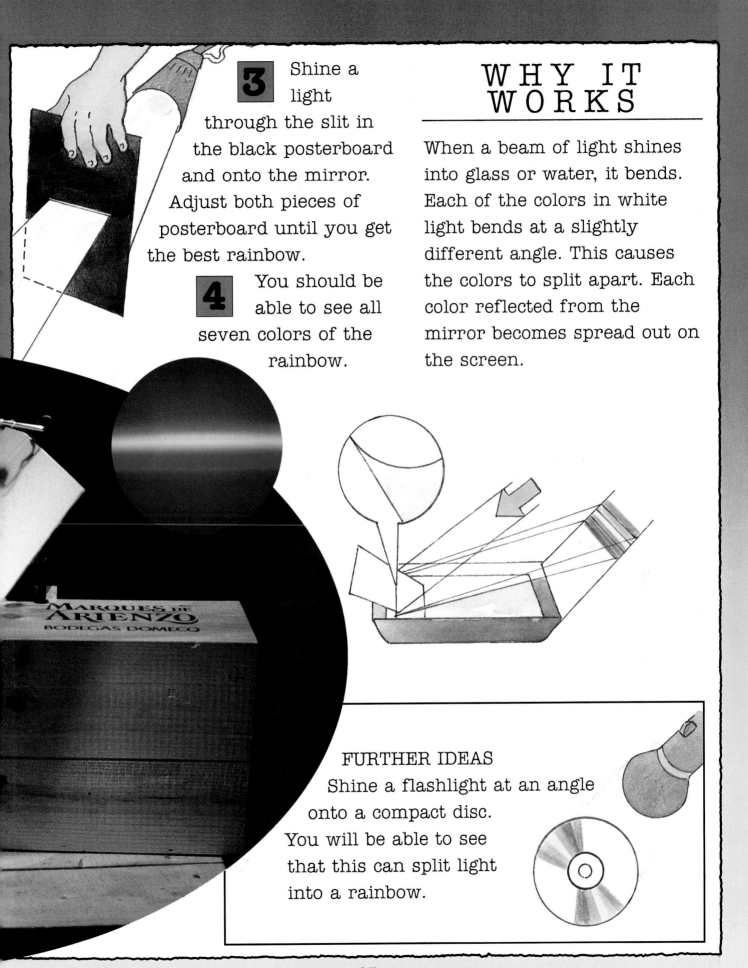

MARQUES DE ARIENZO
BODEGAS DOMECQ

FURTHER IDEAS
Shine a flashlight at an angle onto a compact disc. You will be able to see that this can split light into a rainbow.

MIXING COLORS

Look closely at a color TV or the photographs in this book. The pictures are made up of lots of tiny, colored dots. Because we see books or TV from a distance, the dots seem to mix to make colors.

MAKE A COLOR SPINNER

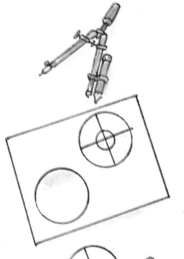

1 Use a pencil and a pair of compasses to draw circles of different sizes onto white posterboard. Cut them out with scissors.

2 Divide the circles into equal sections and decorate each section with different colors. Push a sharp pencil or stick through a hole in the center of each circle.

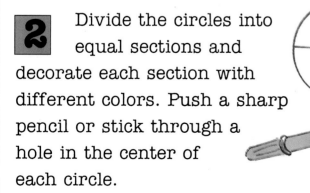

3 Spin the spinner as fast as you can on a tabletop and watch the different colors merge. If you color a spinner with the colors of the rainbow, it may appear white when you spin it.

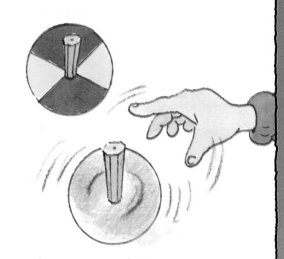

WHY IT WORKS

The spinner is turning so fast that instead of seeing separate colors, our eyes see a mixture. White light is made up of the colors of the rainbow, so a spinner decorated with these colors appears white.

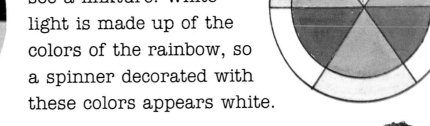

FURTHER IDEAS
Cover three flashlights with red, blue, and green cellophane. Shine them onto white paper (or a white floor). Allow the light beams to overlap. See how many new colors you can make.

SEEING IN THREE-DIMENSION

Animals usually have two eyes. Close one eye and look at an object. Guess how far away it is. Try again with both eyes open. It is much harder to judge distances using only one eye. Having two eyes gives us a sense of depth.

MAKE 3-D GLASSES

1 Measure the distances A and B around your head with a tape measure.

2 Use the distances to draw out your glasses onto cardboard. Cut out the glasses and fold along the dotted lines.

3 Cut out red and green cellophane for the eyeholes. Glue the green over the right eyehole and red over the left. Try on the glasses. Look at the insect picture opposite.

WHY IT WORKS

The left eye covered with red cellophane only sees the green image; the right eye only sees the red. Each eye sees a different view. The brain combines both images to give the illusion of depth.

FURTHER IDEAS

Close one eye. Hold your hands out in front of you at arm's length. Bring your index fingers together so they touch. Can you thread a needle with one eye closed?

SEPARATING COLORS

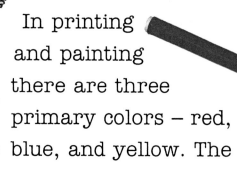

In printing and painting there are three primary colors – red, blue, and yellow. The enormous variety of colored dyes, paints, and inks are made by mixing different amounts of two or more of the primary colors.

FIND THE HIDDEN COLORS

1 With a pair of compasses draw some circles onto paper towels. Cut them out with scissors.

2 Using marker pens, draw a dot of color in the middle of each circle. Black, purple, green, brown, and orange are good colors to use.

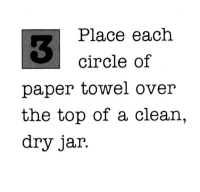

3 Place each circle of paper towel over the top of a clean, dry jar.

4 Add drops of water to the dot of color. Dip a straw into water. Block the top with your finger. Touch the ink dot with the straw.

WHY IT WORKS

Some inks are made up of several colors. These can separate as the water spreads, carrying the colors at different speeds.

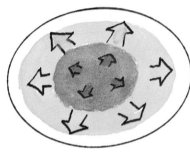

FURTHER IDEAS
Take a long strip of paper towel. Draw a large dot near the bottom. Hang the strip up so the end just dips into a bowl of water. Watch the colors separate as the water rises up the paper.

COLORED DYES

Today we can buy clothes in an enormous variety of colors. These colors come from modern artificial dyes made from oil. Before the nineteenth century, people had always used natural dyes made from plants, animals, or materials in the ground.

TIE–DYE A HANDKERCHIEF

GET AN ADULT TO DO THIS FOR YOU

2 Tie some string around a white cotton handkerchief as tightly as you can.

1 Collect lots of brown onion skins. Ask an adult to boil them in water for 20 minutes.

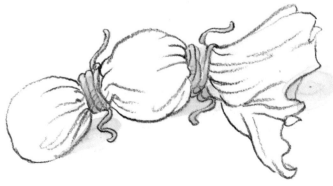

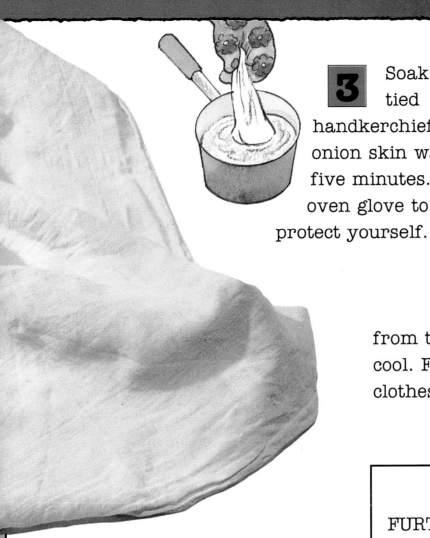

3 Soak the tied handkerchief in the onion skin water for five minutes. Use an oven glove to protect yourself.

4 Cut the string from the dyed handkerchief when cool. Fasten the handkerchief to a clothesline until it is dry.

FURTHER IDEAS
Many vegetables contain different colored pigments. See what color beet juice or spinach water dye fabric.

WHY IT WORKS

Onion skins contain a chemical called a pigment. Boiling brings out the pigment, which in onion skin is yellow. Compare how well the pigment dyes fabrics other than cotton.

COLOR CHANGES

Lemons taste sour because they contain acid ("acid" means sour). Hundreds of chemicals are acidic. It would be very dangerous if scientists had to taste chemicals to identify them. Instead they use a chemical that changes color when acid is added.

GET AN ADULT TO DO THIS FOR YOU

TESTING FOR ACIDS

1 Ask an adult to chop up half a red cabbage. Boil the chopped cabbage in a pan of water for about five minutes.

2 Remove the cabbage from the water. Cut paper towels or filter paper into strips.

3 Dip each strip into the cabbage water. Allow the strips to soak the water up.

4 Let the strips dry. When dry, try adding drops of vinegar, lemon, soap, and other harmless substances to each strip.

WHY IT WORKS

Red cabbage contains a chemical called an indicator. Indicators change color when an acid or alkali is added. Red cabbage juice turns red in acids and green in alkalis. Litmus is an important indicator commonly used by scientists.

5 Note the different colors you see on each strip.

FURTHER IDEAS
You can use geranium petals instead of red cabbage. Geranium petals also contain an indicator that changes color when an acid or alkali is added.

CONTENTS

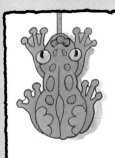

CHAPTER
Two

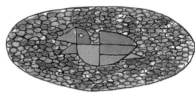

MAKING SHAPES

MYSTERIOUS SHAPES

We can learn a lot about materials and their shapes from nature. All of these shapes are solids, and have at least two sides. What about a one-sided shape? What special properties does it have?

MAKE A MÖBIUS STRIP

1 Color both sides of three paper strips. Tape together the first strip to make a band.

2 Repeat with the second strip, but twist the strip once before sticking the ends together.

WHY IT WORKS

The first strip will make two new bands, the second a single long band and the third, two linked bands. This is a trick of mathematics. The second and third strips are called *Möbius strips*, after their inventor.

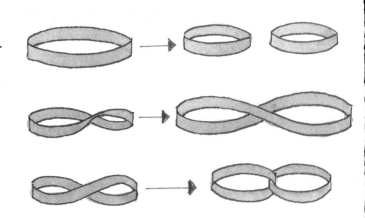

3 Twist the third strip twice before taping the ends together.

4 Finally, cut each band in half lengthwise.

FURTHER IDEAS

Draw a pencil line along each of the bands. You will find that the line continues along both "sides" of the second band!

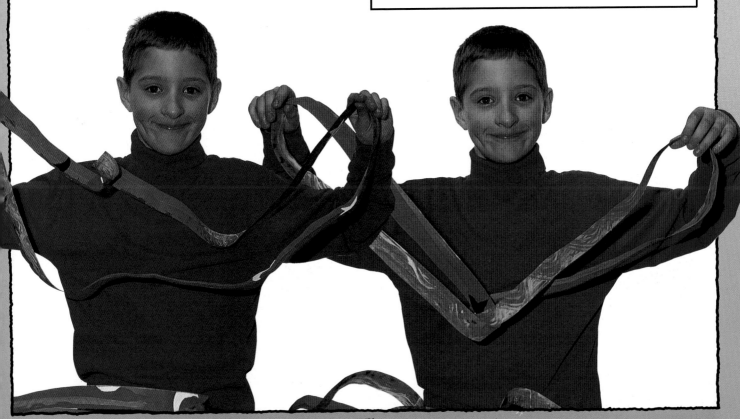

SHAPES IN NATURE

You can find crystals everywhere around you. Gemstones, like emeralds, have always fascinated people. Salt, sand, and sugar are also made from crystals. Then there are the quartz crystals in your watch and the silicon in your computer.

GROW SOME CRYSTALS

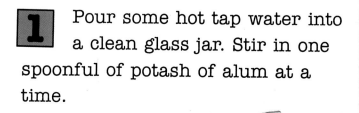

1 Pour some hot tap water into a clean glass jar. Stir in one spoonful of potash of alum at a time.

2 Keep adding alum until no more will dissolve. You now have a *saturated solution*. Leave it for two days.

3 Drain the saturated solution through a strainer. Save the water for later and keep the crystals.

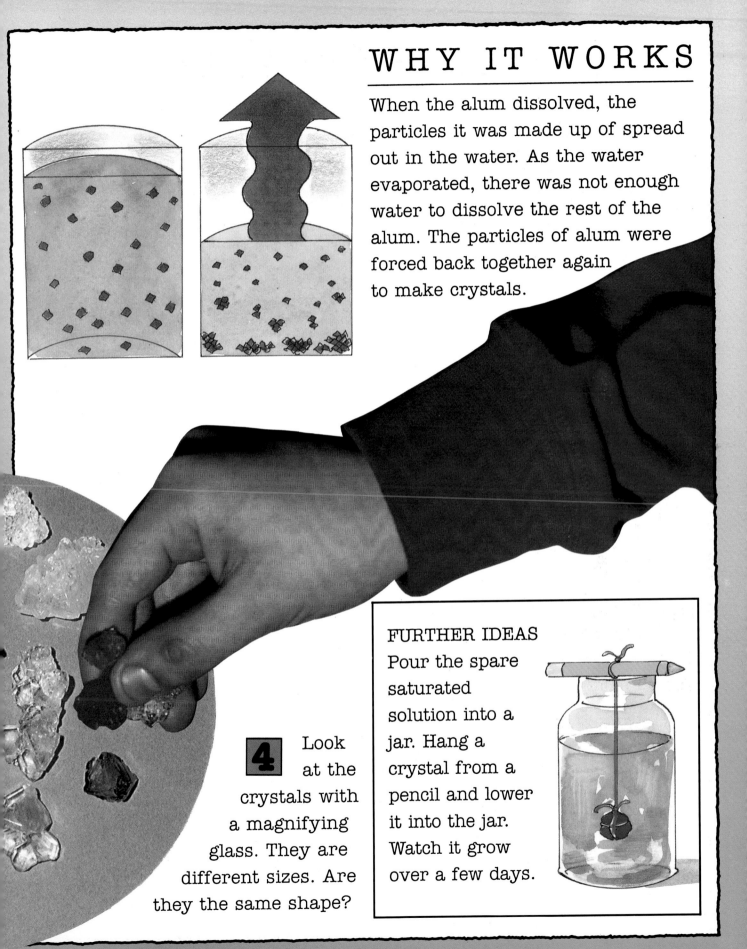

WHY IT WORKS

When the alum dissolved, the particles it was made up of spread out in the water. As the water evaporated, there was not enough water to dissolve the rest of the alum. The particles of alum were forced back together again to make crystals.

4 Look at the crystals with a magnifying glass. They are different sizes. Are they the same shape?

FURTHER IDEAS
Pour the spare saturated solution into a jar. Hang a crystal from a pencil and lower it into the jar. Watch it grow over a few days.

HANGING ROCKS

Rainwater can dissolve some types of solid rock. Sometimes the water drips into an underground cave, leaving a solid behind. Over time this solid slowly builds up to form columns, which hang down from the roof of the cave, called *stalactites*.

GROW A STALACTITE

1 Make a saturated solution with Epsom salts in a jar of hot water.

2 Fill two glasses with the saturated solution.

3 Attach paper clips to the ends of some wool. Hang the ends in the two glasses.

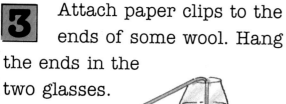

4 Place a saucer under the wool. Leave in a warm, safe place for one week.

5 Watch as the stalactite grows down from the wool to the saucer, over a number of days.

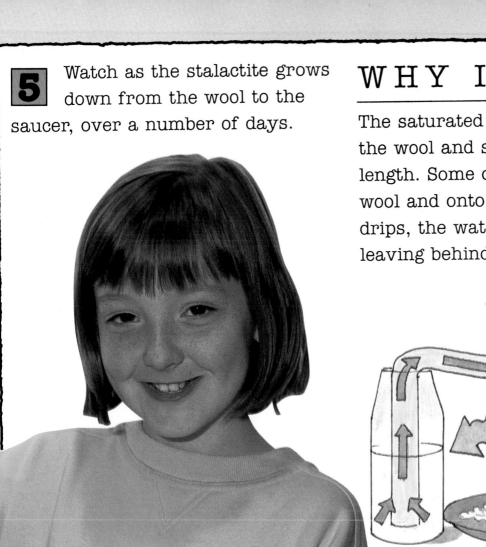

WHY IT WORKS

The saturated solution soaks into the wool and spreads along its length. Some of it drips off the wool and onto the saucer. As it drips, the water evaporates, leaving behind a column of salts.

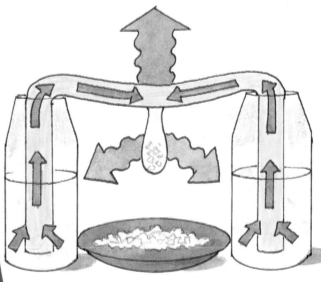

FURTHER IDEAS

Create your own crystalline sculpture. Make a letter by bending a clean pipe cleaner. Dip it into a jar of saturated solution for a few minutes. Leave it to dry slowly.

SHAPE AND STRENGTH

Everybody knows how easy it is to break an egg, because of its very thin shell. However, the egg can also be very strong. It must withstand the impact of falling to the ground when the egg is laid. The egg shape has been produced by nature to be both light and strong.

TEST THE STRENGTH OF AN EGG

1 Find a large tray. Stand up the egg at one side of the tray using clay to hold it in place.

2 At the other side of the tray place two piles of coins exactly the same height as the egg. The egg and two piles should make a triangle.

3 Wrap some books in plastic wrap for protection. Support one book on the coins and egg.

4 Add another book. Watch the egg carefully as you add each book. How many books can the egg help support before it breaks?

WHY IT WORKS

The shape of the egg makes it both hollow and light. It has an arch at each end, a good structure for supporting weight. The egg has a lot of strength lengthwise because the tall arches spread more weight. It is much easier to break when on its side because these arches are weaker.

FURTHER IDEAS
Repeat the test. This time compare the egg's strength to that of some paper shapes, such as a box and a cone.

HANGING AROUND

One of the most important properties of any material is its strength. A material that snaps under the slightest weight is not much use. Nature has made some of the strongest materials around. For example, the silken strands in a spider's web are stronger than steel of the same thickness.

FIND THE STRONGEST STRIP

1 Cut three strips of paper, tissue paper, and plastic from a plastic bag, making them the same length and width.

2 Using tape, fasten a wooden dowel to each end of the strips.

GET AN ADULT TO DO THIS FOR YOU

3 Ask an adult to cut two small holes on each side of the top of three paper cups, to make three baskets.

4 Attach a basket to one of the wooden dowels. Tie string around the other wooden dowel.

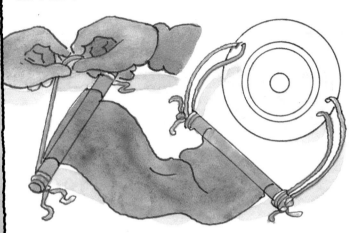

5 Hang each strip from a wall. Slowly add weights to the baskets until each strip breaks.

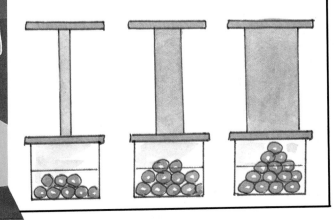

WHY IT WORKS

Plastic is the strongest because its particles are held together by very strong bonds. Paper is made from densely packed fibers that can be split apart quite easily. Tissue paper fibers are not as densely packed, making it the weakest of the three.

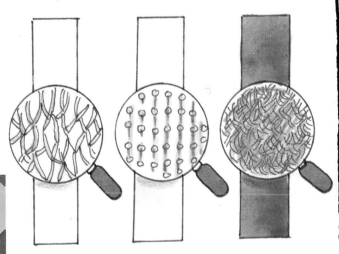

FURTHER IDEAS

Repeat the test with plastic strips of different widths. How does this affect the strength?

MAKING MATERIALS

The materials we find in nature are called *raw materials*. We use many of these and change them to make other products. Glass is made from sand, and paper from wood. We can usually improve a material by changing its properties.

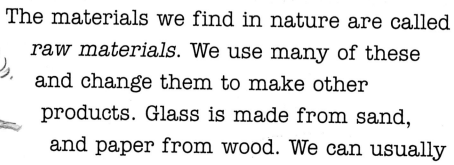

MAKE A PAPIER-MÂCHÉ BOWL

1 Mix some flour and water in a large plastic bowl, keeping the mixture runny.

2 Tear up strips of newspaper, and soak them in the mixture.

3 Inflate a balloon. Starting near the balloon's middle, apply the soaked paper in layers.

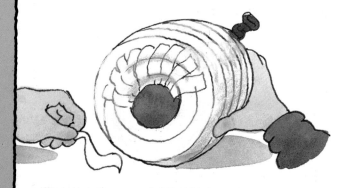

4 To make the bowl's base, sit the balloon on a plastic lid. Cover the lid with more papier-mâché

5 Leave overnight, then remove the balloon. Paint the finished bowl for decoration. Varnish it for extra protection.

WHY IT WORKS

Paper is made up of thousands of tiny strands of wood fibers. The mixture of flour and water fills the gaps between these fibers. As the mixture dries it becomes hard and makes the paper strong and more rigid. It keeps its new shape until soaked again in water.

FURTHER IDEAS

You can use a real bowl as a mold. Cover the bowl with plastic wrap first to make the papier-mâché easy to remove.

FILLING SHAPES

Like papier-mâché, materials such as cement, plaster, and gypsum alter their form when mixed with water and allowed to dry. Unlike papier-mâché, these substances can be poured into molds and used to form shapes, from small statues to enormous buildings.

PLASTER OF PARIS

1 Lubricate the inside of a clean, rubber glove with a few drops of liquid soap.

2 Hang the glove upside down with a couple of clips to hold it open.

3 Use a wooden stick to mix some plaster of Paris with cold water in a glass jar. Mix thoroughly until creamy.

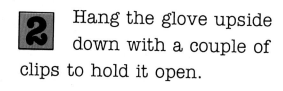

4 Pour the mixture into the glove. Make sure it is filled to the top.

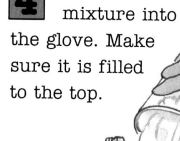

5 Leave overnight to dry out. Gently peel off the glove from the plaster underneath. Be careful! The plaster is quite fragile.

6 Paint the plaster to brighten it up. Use your hand sculpture for holding jewelry.

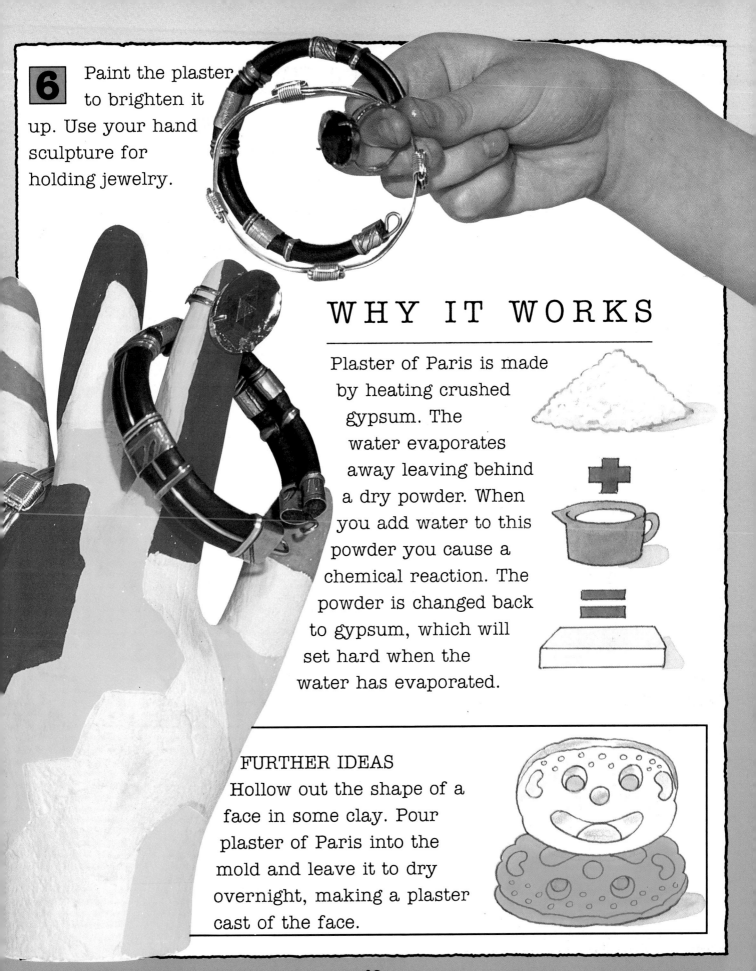

WHY IT WORKS

Plaster of Paris is made by heating crushed gypsum. The water evaporates away leaving behind a dry powder. When you add water to this powder you cause a chemical reaction. The powder is changed back to gypsum, which will set hard when the water has evaporated.

FURTHER IDEAS

Hollow out the shape of a face in some clay. Pour plaster of Paris into the mold and leave it to dry overnight, making a plaster cast of the face.

ELASTIC MATERIALS

One of the reasons metals are so useful is because of their springiness, or *elasticity*. This means that as you pull the material out of shape it tries to return to that shape. Most things have some springiness, especially elastic bands, which are very strong. Glass is also strong, but instead of being elastic it is brittle and shatters.

MAKE A JACK-IN-THE-BOX

1 Ask an adult to coil a piece of stiff wire around a broom handle to make a spring.

2 Cut the neck from a plastic bottle. Attach the spring to the bottom with tape.

3 Ask an adult to secure a lid with paper fasteners.

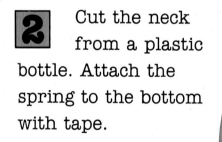

GET AN ADULT TO DO THIS FOR YOU

WHY IT WORKS

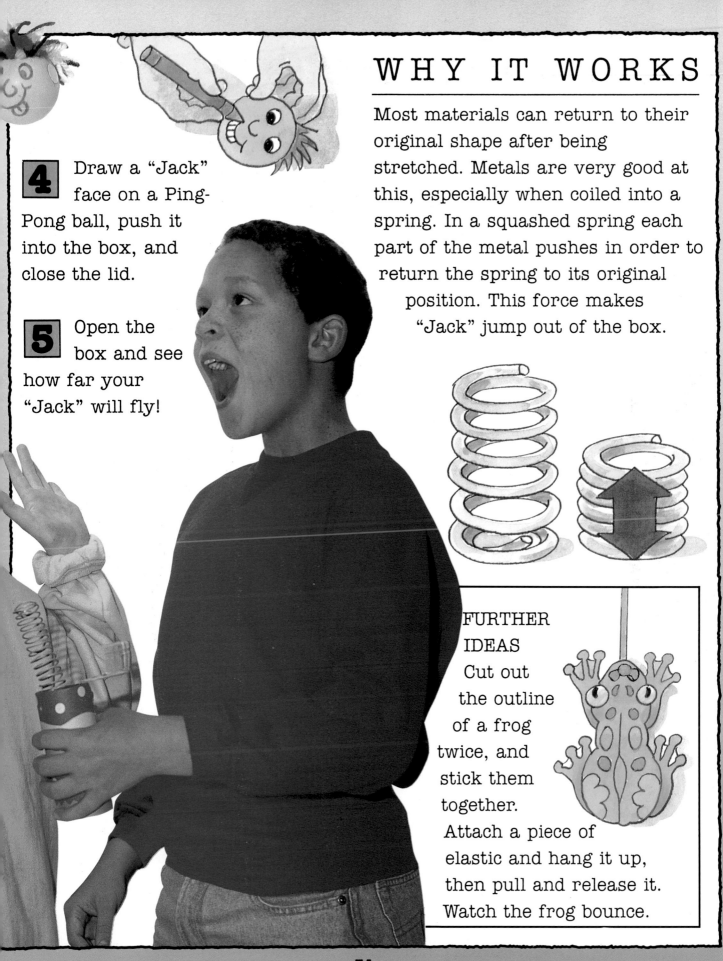

4 Draw a "Jack" face on a Ping-Pong ball, push it into the box, and close the lid.

5 Open the box and see how far your "Jack" will fly!

Most materials can return to their original shape after being stretched. Metals are very good at this, especially when coiled into a spring. In a squashed spring each part of the metal pushes in order to return the spring to its original position. This force makes "Jack" jump out of the box.

FURTHER IDEAS Cut out the outline of a frog twice, and stick them together. Attach a piece of elastic and hang it up, then pull and release it. Watch the frog bounce.

SHAPELESS PLASTICS

Some materials can be pulled into new shapes which they then keep. They do not return to their previous shape as an elastic material would. Such materials are called "plastic." For example, wet clay is plastic because you can mold it into any shape you want and it stays that way.

MAKE SOME PLASTIC MILK

1 Ask an adult to warm some milk in a pan.

2 When the milk starts to boil, slowly stir in a little vinegar.

GET AN ADULT TO HELP YOU WITH THESE

3 Keep stirring. Within seconds the mixture should become rubbery.

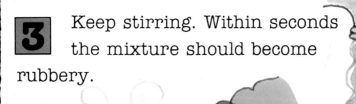

4 Let this rubbery mixture cool. Wash it under the cold water tap, and examine the "plastic."

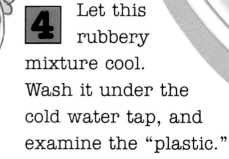

WHY IT WORKS

Vinegar is a member of the chemical family called *acids*. When it is added to the warm milk, it sets up a chemical reaction which rearranges the particles in the milk. Instead of being "runny" and free to move, they clump together. It is this clump that becomes the lump of "plastic."

FURTHER IDEAS
Put a plastic container in a saucepan. Ask an adult to boil water. Pour the boiling water to cover the container, and watch it lose its shape.

FIBERS AND THREADS

Fibers are long, thin, flexible strands of material like threads. Each of your hairs is a fiber. Natural fibers also include animal fur, cotton, and wool. Fibers can be twisted together to make yarn, which can be woven in turn to make fabrics or cloth.

MAKE A LOOM

1 Cut an odd number of notches along the top and bottom of some cardboard.

GET AN ADULT TO DO THIS FOR YOU

2 Wind a piece of string around each pair of notches. Knot it together at the back of the loom.

3 Weave some thick wool across the loom, in and out of the string. To change color, tie another strip to the old one.

4 When you have filled the loom, tie off the last strip of fabric. Lift the weaving off the cardboard.

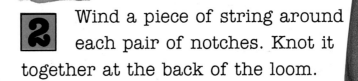

5 Push pieces of a dowel through the top and bottom warp threads. Hang it up as a decoration.

WHY IT WORKS

The strings going up and down are called the *warp threads*. The threads going across are called the *weft threads*. By weaving the threads together the finished fabric is strong. The closer the weave, the stronger the finished fabric.

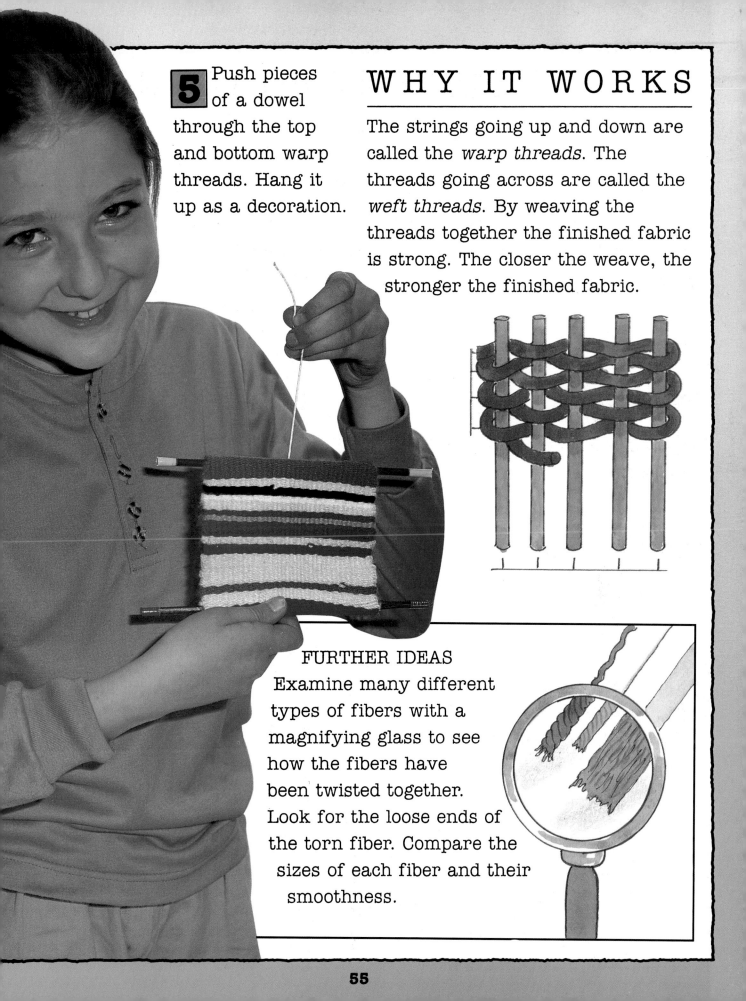

FURTHER IDEAS

Examine many different types of fibers with a magnifying glass to see how the fibers have been twisted together. Look for the loose ends of the torn fiber. Compare the sizes of each fiber and their smoothness.

FITTING IT TOGETHER

Some shapes fit neatly together to cover an area without overlapping or leaving spaces. This is called *tessellation*. Examples are the bricks in a wall and the squares on a chessboard. An example in nature is the honeycomb in a beehive, where hexagonal cells fit snugly together.

MAKE A TRIANGLE PUZZLE

1 On a large sheet of white cardboard, draw a triangle with sides 12 inches long.

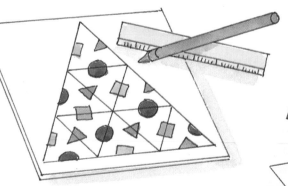

2 Divide the large triangle into nine smaller ones. Each side should be 4 inches long.

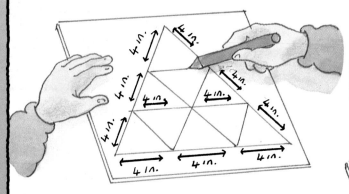

3 On each of the triangles draw a circle, a square, and a triangle as shown.

GET AN ADULT TO HELP YOU WITH THIS

4 Use sharp scissors to carefully cut out each of the nine small triangles.

WHY IT WORKS

A tessellated structure, like a beehive, must have no gaps or overlapping shapes. Only certain shapes, such as triangles and hexagons, will tessellate. To cover a surface with circles, which do not tessellate, you would have to overlap the shapes, or leave gaps.

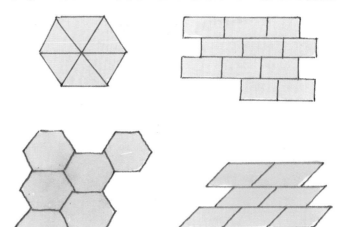

5 Challenge a friend with your triangle puzzle. They should be able to match up the pattern to correctly put the big triangle back together again.

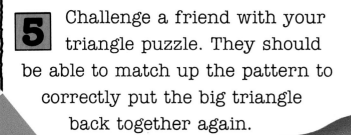

FURTHER IDEAS
A mosaic is like a tessellation, but the shapes that fit together are not the same. Cut out alot of small cardboard shapes. Glue them down to fit the outline of a drawing on cardboard. Make the gaps as small as possible.

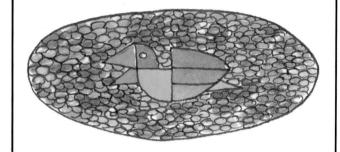

BRIDGES

Since earliest times people have built bridges to cross rivers and other obstacles. The first bridges were probably tree trunks laid across a stream. Later, bridges were built from arches to carry heavier loads. Modern bridges use either steel girders or suspension cables, for support.

BUILD MODEL BRIDGES

1 Find six blocks of wood to make three bridges. Tape pencils to two of the corners on each block.

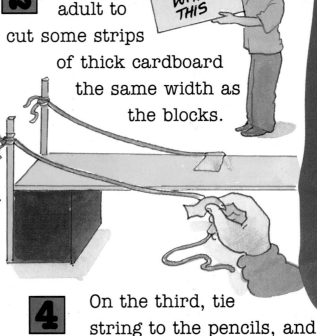

2 Ask an adult to cut some strips of thick cardboard the same width as the blocks.

GET AN ADULT TO HELP YOU WITH THIS

3 Place a strip of cardboard between two blocks to make a beam bridge. With the second, use an arch as a support.

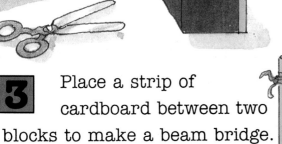

4 On the third, tie string to the pencils, and tape the string to the strip to make a suspension bridge.

5 Draw a river on a sheet of cardboard. Place it under your bridges.

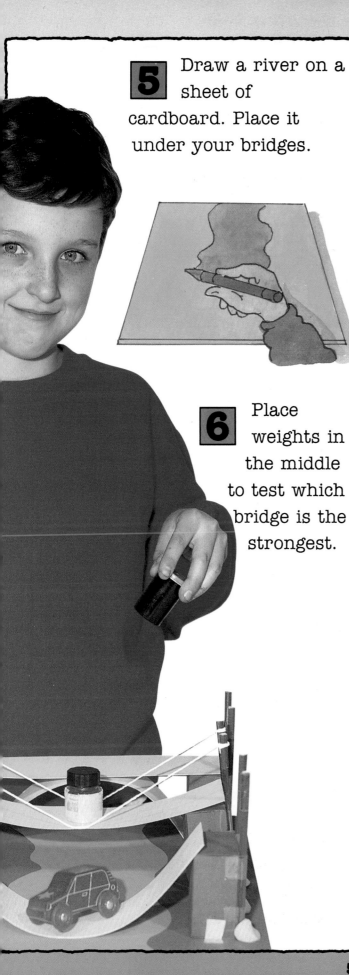

6 Place weights in the middle to test which bridge is the strongest.

WHY IT WORKS

The beam bridge is the weakest because the weight is not spread. The string in the suspension bridge takes some of the weight. The arch is strongest because the weight is spread out over its whole length.

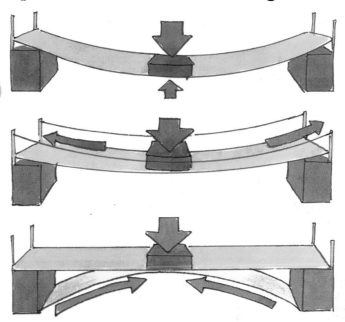

FURTHER IDEAS
Try making a bridge frame out of plastic straws. Join the straws together by pushing the end of one into another.

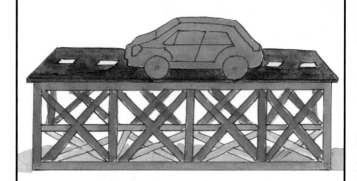

CONTENTS

CHAPTER
Three

PUSHING
AND
PULLING

WHAT IS A FORCE?

If you want to make anything move you have to give it a push or a pull. Scientists call this push or pull a force. Sir Isaac Newton was inspired to write about the force of gravity after an apple landed on his head. The unit of force is called a newton – roughly the force or weight of one apple!

MAKE A FORCE METER

1 Cut out three rectangles from a thick sheet of cardboard. Tape two together to make a "T." Tape the third to support the base.

2 Make a small hole near the top of the cardboard. Push through a wooden dowel about six inches long. Secure firmly.

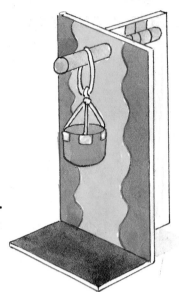

3 Find a circular-shaped box or can. Attach two strong threads to the box.

Hang the threads from a paper clip.

4 Loop a rubber band through the paper clip. Hang the box from the wooden dowel using the rubber band.

5 Place one object at a time in the box. Note how far the rubber band stretches.

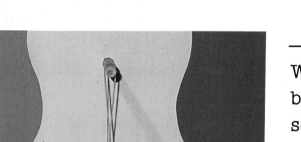

WHY IT WORKS

We can measure how big forces are by seeing how far the rubber band stretches each time. The band must return to its original length after each stretch.

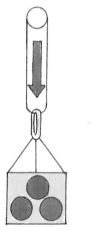

FURTHER IDEAS

Measure the forces made by your own muscles with a set of bathroom scales. Squeeze as hard as you can and check how far the scale goes around. Can you push as hard as your own weight?

63

THE PULL OF GRAVITY

Gravity is the mysterious force: Everybody knows it is there but it is very difficult to understand. Planet Earth keeps everything attracted to it quite firmly, because of the pull of gravity. When you see pictures of astronauts floating around in space apparently weightless, they are not being subjected to the Earth's pull of gravity.

RACE WITH GRAVITY

1 Lay a 12-inch ruler flat on a sheet of white cardboard. Use a pencil to draw a line all around the ruler.

2 Use a pair of scissors to carefully cut out the shape from the cardboard.

3 Divide the cardboard into six equal parts. Color each part brightly with markers.

4 Ask a friend to hold the cardboard hanging down just above your outstretched hand. When your friend releases it, try to catch the cardboard as quickly as you can.

WHY IT WORKS

This is a race between gravity and your body. By the time the message has traveled from your brain to your hand, gravity has pulled the cardboard down by many inches.

FURTHER IDEAS

Ask a friend to drop a small (Ping-Pong) ball down a cardboard tube. Hold a ruler ready near the bottom of the tube. You have to swat the ball before it hits the ground.

BALANCING WEIGHT

We take the art of balance for granted once we have learned to walk as babies. Tightrope walkers have only the thin rope keeping them in the air. Everyone marvels as they balance carefully and defy gravity. This takes great skill as well as courage.

MAKE A BALANCING MAN

1 Draw a "man" shape onto some thick white cardboard. Carefully cut out the shape with scissors.

2 Color in the man to make him look more human. Carefully glue a thumbtack to the bottom of the cardboard.

3 Ask an adult to cut off a piece of coat hanger wire. Glue it into place.

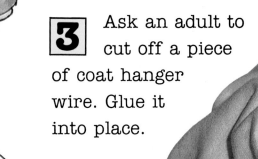

4 Make two small clay balls of the same size. Wrap one ball around each end of the wire.

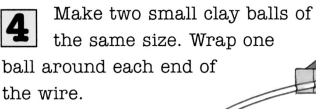

5 Carefully stand the balancing man on top of a bottle. He may wobble slightly but should keep his balance.

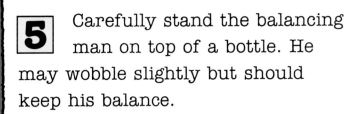

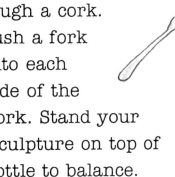

WHY IT WORKS

Gravity keeps everything resting on the ground. In this experiment most of the pulling force of gravity is due to the two heavy balls. It is because these balls are low that the man has a low center of gravity. Any object will balance when its center of gravity is low.

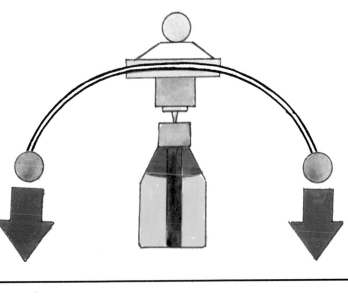

FURTHER IDEAS

You can make a simpler balancing sculpture. Ask an adult to stick a long pin through a cork. Push a fork into each side of the cork. Stand your sculpture on top of a bottle to balance.

SMALL WEIGHTS

You probably see people weighing goods every time you go shopping. They expect to pay only for what they get. "How much" you have of something is normally measured by its weight. Everything has weight, no matter how small, because of the pull of gravity.

MAKE A MICROBALANCE

1 Cut some thick cardboard into this diamond shape. Fold along the dotted lines.

2 Cut out this shape (slightly over three times the width of a drinking straw) twice from cardboard. Fold into triangular shapes and slide one over each end of a straw.

3 Fold the thick cardboard diamond into a support. Push a steel pin through the cardboard and straw. Strengthen the base with tape.

4 Glue the triangular shapes to the ends of the straw. Make sure they balance each other.

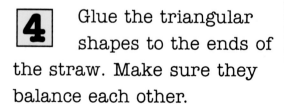

5 Remove the front of a cardboard box to screen your microbalance from drafts. Compare the weights of small objects like a pea or bean.

WHY IT WORKS

The heavier an object is, the bigger the force of gravity tugging on it. The side of the straw that is pulled harder will tilt down. When the weights on both sides are equal, then the two forces balance out.

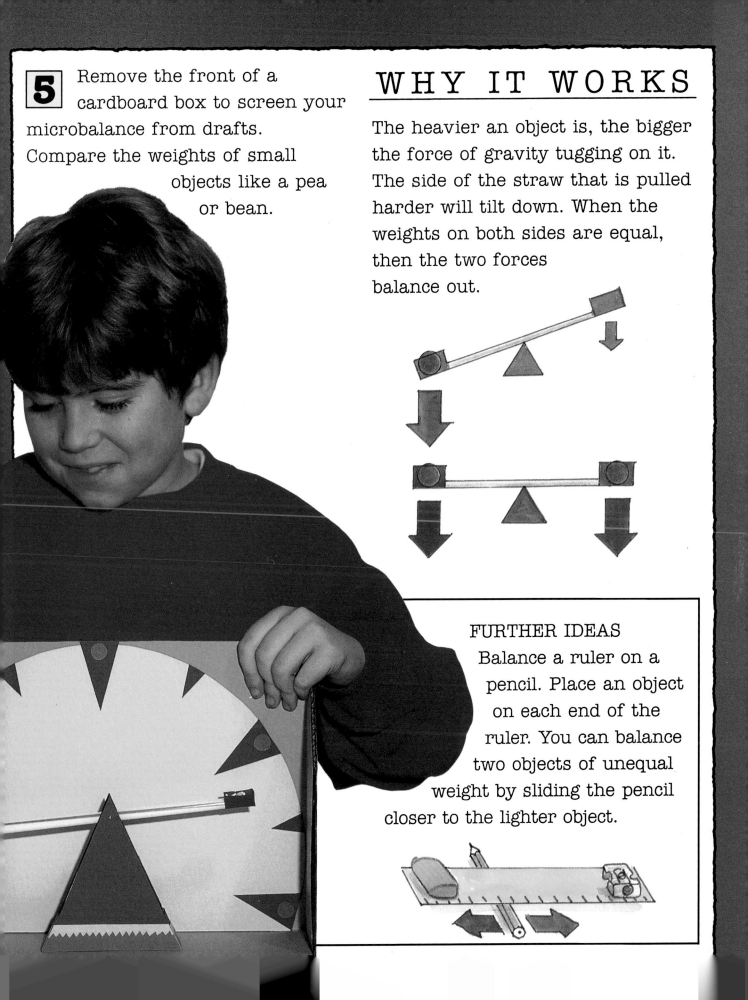

FURTHER IDEAS
Balance a ruler on a pencil. Place an object on each end of the ruler. You can balance two objects of unequal weight by sliding the pencil closer to the lighter object.

FRICTION

Whenever any two things rub against each other, the force of friction tries to stop them. Rubbing your hands together warms them because of friction. Friction is useful because without it there would be no grip! Things would just slip and slide away from each other. Friction can also be a problem because it causes things to overheat.

MEASURING FRICTION

1 Draw the seven shapes A to G on thick cardboard. Carefully cut them out. They will be the parts of your ramp.

2 Fold shape A along the dotted lines into a prism and stand it on shape C. Tape shape E to shape C. Position shape D between shapes A and E.

3 Fold shape B along the dotted lines into a box. Position it at the end of the ramp. Glue shapes F and G into place. Flip up shape D to make your runway (shape E) steeper.

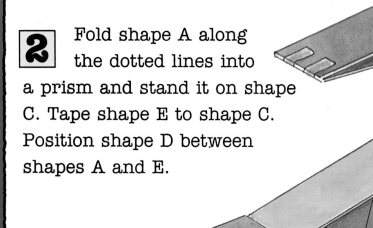

WHY IT WORKS

4 Place a coin at the top of the runway.
Slowly make the runway steeper until the coin slides down. Compare with a wooden block, an eraser, and a cork.

There is more friction, or grip, between rough surfaces than between smooth ones. Even though the eraser and the cardboard feel smooth, they have tiny rough edges. Only when the runway is steep enough, can this grip between eraser and cardboard be overcome.

FURTHER IDEAS

Cut out a piece of aluminum foil to fit your runway. Carefully lay it flat and into place. Repeat your tests. Is there more friction from the aluminum compared to the cardboard? Compare other surfaces, such as: felt, plastic, or paper. Can you tell which surface has the most friction?

GETTING A GRIP

Grip is very important to drivers. The wheels of a vehicle can slide, especially on slippery surfaces like mud, and may cause an accident. Tractors' wheels are very big and knobbly to increase their grip on muddy fields.

MAKE A SPOOL TRACTOR

1 Ask an adult to remove the wick from a candle and cut off a disc from the end of the candle.

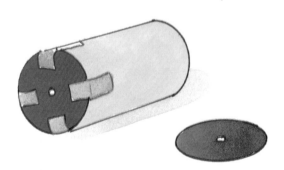

2 Cut out two circles of cardboard to fit the ends of a spool of thread. Make a small hole in the center and tape each into place.

3 Thread a small rubber band through the wax disc. Stop it from going all the way through by looping the end around a pencil.

4 Thread the other end of the rubber band through the spool. A straightened paper clip will help with threading. Attach the end of the rubber band to half of a matchstick.

5 Wind up the pencil tightly without breaking the rubber band. Place the tractor on the floor, and let the matchstick push it along.

WHY IT WORKS

The wound up rubber band stores energy. As the rubber band starts to unwind, it makes the pencil rotate. The matchstick presses against the ground. Since one end of the matchstick cannot move against the ground, the energy is used up by making the spool of thread rotate instead. This is what pushes the tractor forward.

FURTHER IDEAS
Wrap rubber bands around the spool to act as rubber tires and improve the grip. See what is the steepest slope it can climb up. (Use the friction tester on pp 70 and 71).

HYDRAULIC FORCES

Powerful machines like cranes, forklifts, and fire engines use hydraulic forces to lift heavy things quite easily. "Hydro" means water, although in practice these machines use other liquids in their hydraulics.

MAKE A HYDRAULIC FORCE

1 Ask an adult to cut the necks off two large plastic bottles, then to cut a hole near the bottom of each.

2 Thread a plastic tube through the bottles. Tie the neck of a balloon over one end of the tube. Fill the other end of the tube with water.

3 Fill another balloon with water. Tie this balloon to the free end of the tube. Both balloons and the tube must be filled with water.

4 Find two empty cans that just fit into the bottles. Place them above the balloons. Gently push down on one can with the palm of your hand.

5 The second can rises by the same distance that you pressed down the first. You can reverse this by pressing down on the second can.

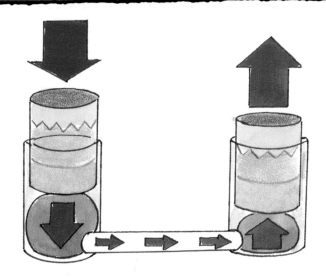

WHY IT WORKS

It is very difficult to squash water. If you squeeze it hard in one place, it will push out just as hard in another place. The water transmits the force from one can to the other. This is the principle used by all hydraulic machines.

FURTHER IDEAS

Glue a small plastic toy to a balloon. Connect the balloon to a plastic syringe with a tube. Lay the balloon flat in a glass tumbler and inflate with the syringe. This pump uses air, which is springy compared to water, to make the balloon inflate.

WHAT A DRAG!

It is quite hard to move quickly under the water. The water gets in your way and before you can move forward you must push it out of the way. The water exerts a special force of friction called "drag." Birds and airplanes have wings designed to reduce "drag" in the air.

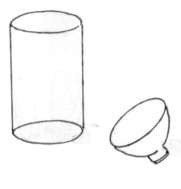

TESTING MOVING SHAPES

1 Find a large plastic bottle and ask an adult to cut off the neck. Otherwise use a long plastic tube.

2 Find a small but sturdy box. Cut a piece of thick cardboard and tape it to the back of the box.

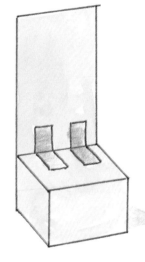

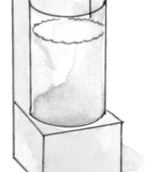

3 Use a funnel to carefully fill the bottle with cooking oil. Stand the bottle on the box.

4 Mold the same amount of clay into different shapes. Attach a piece of cotton to each shape.

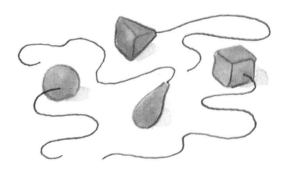

5 Hold the shapes just above the bottle, release, and start timing. Make sure you hold on to the cotton. Stop timing when the shapes reach the bottom.

WHY IT WORKS

Cooking oil has more drag than water so it is easier to see how much the shapes are slowed down. A shape has to push the oil out of its path to move forward. Shapes with a rounded front allow liquids to pass around them with little drag.

FURTHER IDEAS

Try some of these shapes. Predict which will move the fastest before you test them. Add a small weight to the front of each shape to stop it from turning around as it falls.

PULLEYS

A pulley is a machine to help you lift very heavy loads. Cranes are useful machines with a system of pulleys that make lifting heavy objects easier. You can see cranes almost everywhere – on building sites, at docks and railroad stations.

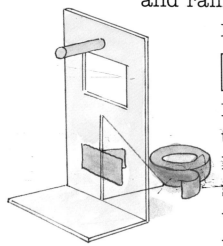

MAKE A SIMPLE PULLEY

1 Cut out a window from cardboard. Fold it and tape a triangle to the back to help it stand up. Push a short wooden dowel through the top.

2 Cut four circles of cardboard, each with a hole in the middle. Push a piece of straw through each pair of circles.

3 Bend three pieces of thin wire into shape. Attach the circles to the wire to make one double pulley and one single pulley.

4 Hang the pulleys as shown. Make sure you loop the thread around the lower pulley, back over the top pulley, and out through the window.

5 Hang a small weight from the hook on the lower pulley. Pull the thread from behind the window to lift the weight.

WHY IT WORKS

A pulley system allows a force to be transferred from one place to another. As you pull on the thread, the force is transferred along the thread all the way to the weight. You can lift the weight with half the effort but it only moves half the distance.

FURTHER IDEAS

Make a winch from a cardboard base and clay-filled straw. Hold the straw in place with wire. Wrap thread around the straw, and tie a hook to the other end. Attach weights to the hook and pull them in by winding the winch.

AROUND AND AROUND

Electric mixers, washing machines, and dryers all operate by spinning forces. A gyroscope is a terrific toy that seems to defy gravity while it spins. The spinning force balances out the force of gravity and makes the spinning object hard to push over.

MAKE SPINNING TOPS

1 Find a large sheet of thin white cardboard. Use a pair of compasses to draw some circles of different sizes.

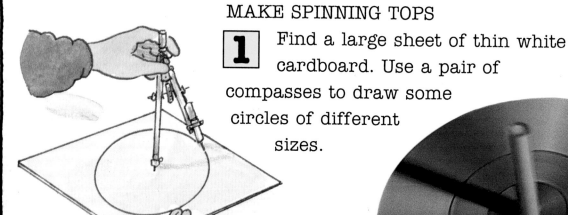

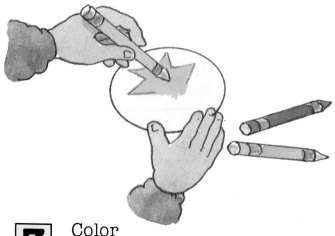

2 Use a pair of scissors to cut out each circle carefully.

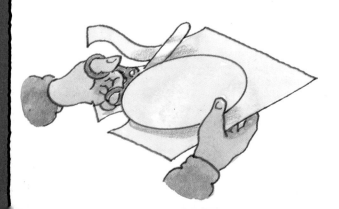

3 Color each circle with bright markers. Create a different design for each one.

4 Make a small hole through the center of each circle. Then push a sharp pencil through each hole.

WHY IT WORKS

When you start the top spinning, you give it a lot of spinning energy. The top spins for minutes before this energy is all used up. The top actually stores some of the energy during this time so that it can go on spinning. The energy you gave it is only gradually released.

5 Hold the top of the pencil between two fingers and spin it as fast as you can. Release it and let it spin on a smooth tabletop.

FURTHER IDEAS
Place an egg on a plate and start it spinning fast. Suddenly grab the egg to stop its spinning. Quickly release it and it will start spinning again all by itself!

TRANSFERRING FORCES

All of the power in a modern car comes from the engine. The forces made by the engine are then transferred to where they are needed – mainly to make the wheels turn. One of the most common ways of transferring forces is through gearwheels.

MAKE MODEL GEARS

1 Draw and cut out four equal circles with teeth all the way around them using thick cardboard. These are your gearwheels.

2 Make a small hole in the middle of each wheel. Add another close to the middle of one wheel. Draw and cut out the other shapes shown here.

3 Use a thumbtack to attach one wheel to a piece of cardboard. Insert an extra piece of cardboard between the cardboard and paper clip for a tight fit.

4 Attach the other wheel to the bar and hammer with a thumbtack. Attach these to the first wheel so that the teeth match.

5 Rotate the upper wheel slowly. Watch how the hammer moves from side to side.

WHY IT WORKS

As you turn the first gearwheel, this turning movement is passed on to the second gearwheel. The bar moves from side to side as the wheel turns and this sets up the sideways movement of the hammer.

FURTHER IDEAS
Try using different-sized wheels in your gear system. Notice how they move at different speeds: The larger gears move more slowly than the smaller gears.

EQUAL AND OPPOSITE

Forces always come in pairs. When a cannon fires a shell, the cannon itself recoils. The force pushing the shell FORWARD has an equal but opposite force.

MAKE A JET ENGINE

1 Cut out these shapes from thin cardboard. Tape the strip into a circle. Attach a drinking straw.

2 Tape together all of the shapes to make up the outline of a rocket like the one illustrated below.

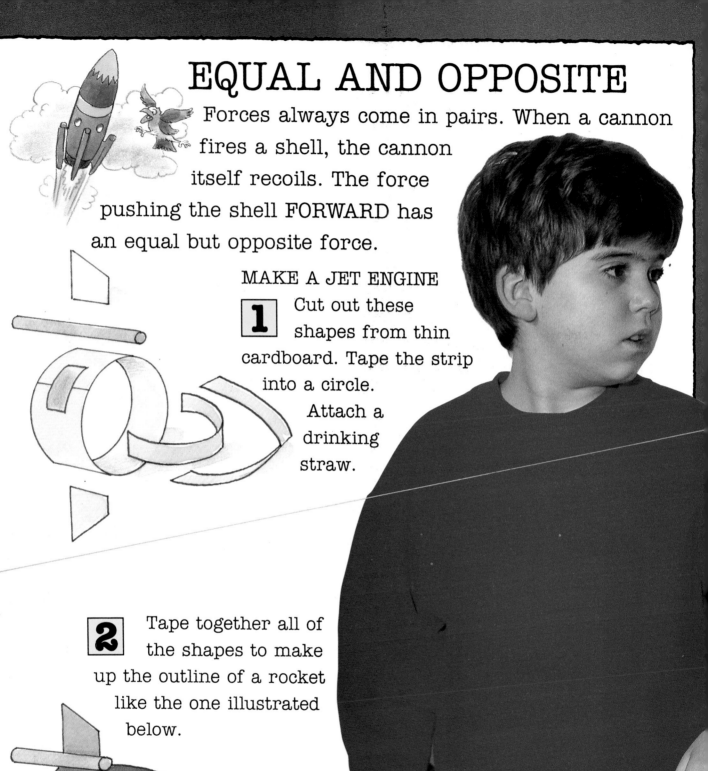

3 Place a balloon in the cardboard. Slowly inflate it until it is a tight fit inside the rocket outline. Keep holding the neck of the balloon.

4 Thread string through the straw. Fasten the ends of the string across the room. Release the balloon to be jet-propelled along the string.

WHY IT WORKS

Over 300 years ago, Sir Isaac Newton found that every force has an equal but opposite reaction. As the air rushes out of the back of your balloon in one direction, the balloon itself is pushed forward in the opposite direction. This is the principle on which all jet engines work.

FURTHER IDEAS
Sit in a chair with wheels, and hold a soccerball. Try to throw it without moving. The harder you throw it, the stronger is the opposite force that pushes you backward.

CONTENTS

CHAPTER *Four*

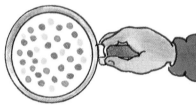

MAKING THINGS CHANGE

FREEZING AND MELTING

When the weather becomes cold, it can change many of the things around us. It can cause water to freeze, or solidify, into ice or snow. This change is easy to reverse; warmed ice will thaw, or melt, back into water.

EXPANDING ICE

1 Find two large empty plastic bottles. Tape a paper marker around each about half way up.

2 Using a large pitcher of water, carefully fill each of the bottles exactly to the mark on the paper.

3 Place one bottle in a warm room and the other in your freezer. Leave them overnight.

4 Take out the frozen bottle and compare the water level in each of them.

WHY IT WORKS

There seems to be more ice. This is because water expands, gets larger, when it freezes. Pipes sometimes burst in winter because the water inside freezes and expands.

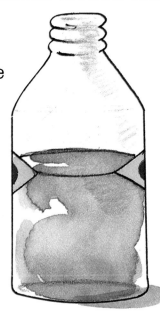

FURTHER IDEAS
Find lumps of chocolate, butter and wax from a candle, about the same size as an ice cube. Place them on a tray. Leave the tray in a warm place to compare how they melt. Place the tray in the freezer to reverse the changes.

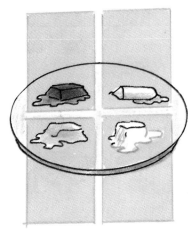

THE ACID TEST

Chemicals are split into families of *acids*, *alkalis* or *neutrals*. These chemicals are everywhere – even in soil. The color of the Hydrangea flower depends on the levels of acid or alkali in the soil. Blue flowers mean there is more acid in the soil; pink, more alkali.

MAKE A CHEMICAL INDICATOR

1 Take a red cabbage, tear it into shreds, and place these shreds into a bowl.

GET AN ADULT TO HELP YOU WITH THIS

2 Pour hot water into the bowl. The cabbage color dissolves to make an indicator.

3 Strain the juice, and pour the liquid into three small jars.

WHY IT WORKS

A chemical that changes color in acids and alkalis is called an indicator. Red cabbage juice turns red when in acids, like vinegar, and green when in alkalis, like soap.

4 Add a different liquid to each jar, such as vinegar or liquid soap. Compare the colors.

FURTHER IDEAS
Make indicator paper by soaking blotting paper in the indicator. Then test household items.

BUBBLES AND FIZZ

Carbon dioxide is the gas in carbonated drinks which keeps them full of bubbles. When you shake a carbonated drink, then suddenly release the cap, the gas inside bubbles up and escapes. Carbon dioxide gas is important in other ways. It can be used to put out fires and it also makes cakes rise. Here you can make your own bubbles of gas.

MAKE AN ERUPTING VOLCANO

1 Find a small glass jar. Stand it on a saucer. This will be your volcano.

2 Cover the sides of the jar with clay to make the volcano.

3 Carefully fill half the jar with baking soda. Add a few drops of red food coloring. Then add vinegar, a spoonful at a time.

4 Stand back and watch as the mixture bubbles up and over the sides of the volcano.

WHY IT WORKS

A mixture of the acid in vinegar and alkali in baking soda makes bubbles of gas. The thousands of bubbles are very light and this causes the mixture to fizz. The eruption of bubbles is similar to lava erupting from a volcano.

FURTHER IDEAS
Fill a glass with vinegar and add a tablespoonful of baking soda. Drop in mothballs. Bubbles of gas make them rise back to the surface.

PRETTY FLOWERS

Plants, like animals, need water to stay alive. The roots of plants are especially good at taking water from the ground. Water moves through the plant in tiny tubes, which are similar to the blood vessels in an animal.

CHANGE FLOWER COLORS

1 Fill three glass bottles with water. Add a few drops of different food coloring to each.

2 Find three freshly cut flowers, preferably white or light-colored.

3 Trim the stem of each flower before placing them into the three bottles.

4 Leave the flowers overnight. Each becomes the color of the water in which it was placed.

WHY IT WORKS

Water travels up the stem of each flower and spreads to all parts of the plant, including the petals. The water then escapes from the plant into the air by evaporation. Fresh water is continually drawn up to replace the lost water.

FURTHER IDEAS

Repeat with a fresh stalk of celery. When the water has risen through it, ask an adult to slice the stalk. With a magnifying glass you should see the thin tubes that carry the water.

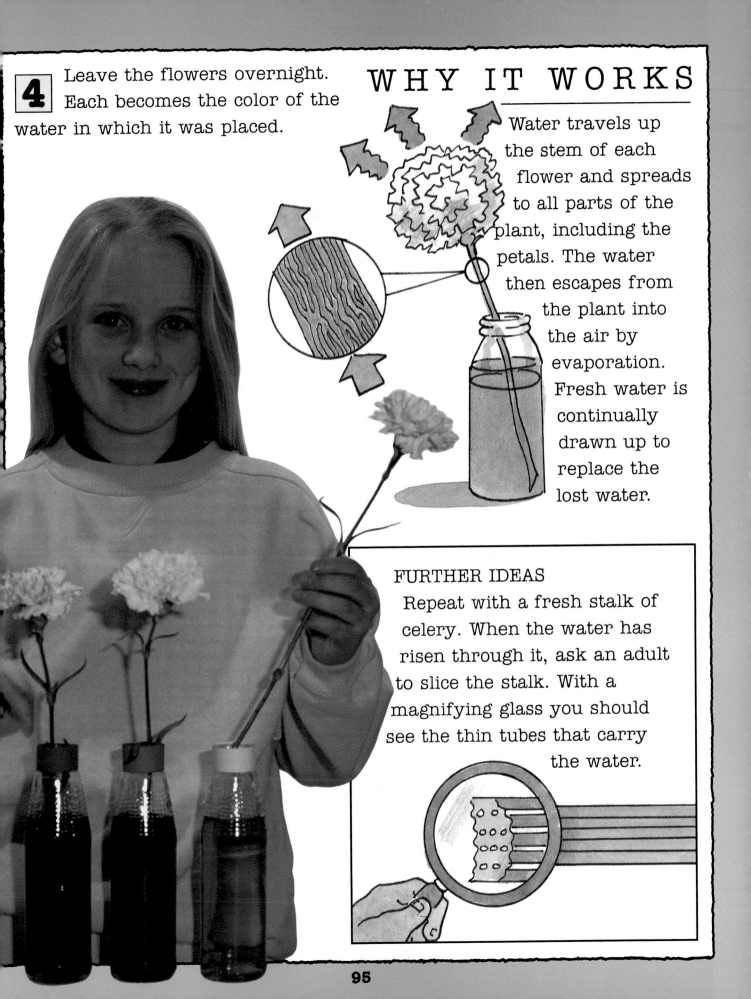

FLOWING CURRENTS

Currents of hot air rise from warm valleys to the cooler hilltops. These are called *thermals*. They are very useful to hot air balloons, gliders, and even birds. The rising warm air helps to keep them aloft.

SEE HOT WATER CURRENTS

1 Find a small jar with a metal screw-on lid. Ask an adult to make some small holes in the lid.

GET AN ADULT TO DO THIS FOR YOU

2 Tie a piece of string tightly around the neck of the jar. Make sure the string can support the jar.

3 Place a few drops of food coloring in the jar and fill it with hot water. Screw the lid on tightly.

96

4 Fill a glass jug with cold water. Holding the string, gently lower the jar into the glass jug.

5 Watch as the colored water swirls around in the cold water.

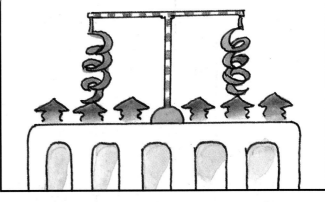

WHY IT WORKS

Hot liquids expand and become less dense than the cold liquid around them. This causes the hot liquid to rise into the jug. Eventually the heat is spread out, and the cooled, denser liquid sinks to the bottom of the pitcher. This movement of the liquid is known as a *convection current.*

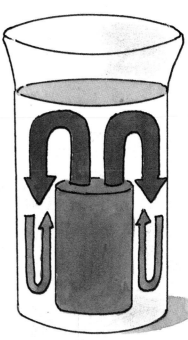

FURTHER IDEAS
Cut out some strips from circles of paper. Hold them above a heater. Rising warm air causes the strips to rotate.

RISING TEMPERATURES

On a hot day, you can see the temperature rise if you watch a thermometer carefully. As the air gets hotter, the liquid inside the thermometer expands up the glass tube. All liquids expand when heated, but usually only by a tiny amount.

MAKE A BOTTLE FOUNTAIN

1 Find a small glass jar with a screw-on lid. Fill the jar half full with cold water. Add a few drops of food coloring.

GET AN ADULT TO HELP YOU WITH THIS

2 Ask an adult to make a hole in the lid just big enough for a thin straw. Seal the straw in place with some clay.

3 Plug the end of the straw with clay. Use a pin to make a tiny hole in the plug.

4 Fill a large bowl with hot tap water. Stand the small jar upside-down in the bowl on some clay, with the straw sticking above the water level.

5 Wait for the small jar to heat up, and stand back to admire the fountain of colored water spraying out of the top.

WHY IT WORKS

The heat from the hot water bowl warms up the air inside the jar, and this air expands. As it does so, it pushes on the water below. The water can only escape one way – by spraying out of the top of the straw.

FURTHER IDEAS
Fill a jar with water. Put a straw through a hole in the lid and seal with clay. Turn the jar upside-down. See how the level in the straw changes when the jar is put in hot water and in a refrigerator.

SEPARATING MIXTURES

Tap water has been filtered many times to remove all impurities before you drink it. Filtering is like straining; it is a way of purifying a liquid by removing any solids that do not dissolve naturally.

MAKE MUDDY WATER CLEAR

1 Mix some mud, clay, or soil with water in a jar. Make a cone shape out of a coffee filter.

2 Carefully place the cone in the neck of a clean glass jar. Slowly pour the muddy mixture through the cone.

3 See how much clearer the filtered water appears. Warning: Do not drink the filtered water – it still contains germs.

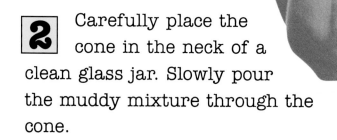

WHY IT WORKS

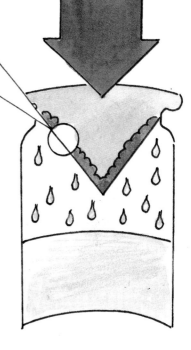

There are tiny holes in the paper that only allow water droplets to squeeze through. The pieces of solid are larger and get trapped.

FURTHER IDEAS

Dissolve some salt in a tall, clean glass of water. Leave it in a warm place for a few days. See how salt is left behind when all the water has evaporated.

RUST OR BUST

Though many metals are strong, tough materials, they do not last forever. When iron is constantly damp it will rust; pieces of iron turn brown and crumble away. Rust can be a terrible problem. It can attack your car, bicycle, or anything else made from iron. The iron is changed into a new chemical that we call *rust*, or "iron oxide."

A RUST RACE

1 Set up five glass jars with some steel wool in each. Add nothing to the first jar. Fill half the second jar with tap water. Fill the third to the brim with boiled water and tighten the lid. In the fourth, put the steel wool on a piece of damp cloth. Put tap water in the last jar, and add a pinch of salt.

2 Leave the jars for at least a week. Regularly examine the steel wool for signs of rust.

WHY IT WORKS

So-called "steel wool" is really made of iron. The steel wool rusts in jars 2 and 4, but especially in jar 5. Iron needs water and air to rust. The air and water particles attach to the iron particles to form iron oxide. Boiled water has no air in it. Salt makes iron rust faster.

FURTHER IDEAS
Scratch away some of the surface of some empty cans. See if the cans rust when damp.

INVISIBLE INK

Have you ever wanted to write a secret message that only you can read? This project lets you write your message on a sheet of paper. When you have finished, the message is invisible – the paper just looks blank. Nobody can read it unless they know the method for making the message visible.

SEND A SECRET MESSAGE

1 Squeeze some lemon juice into a glass.

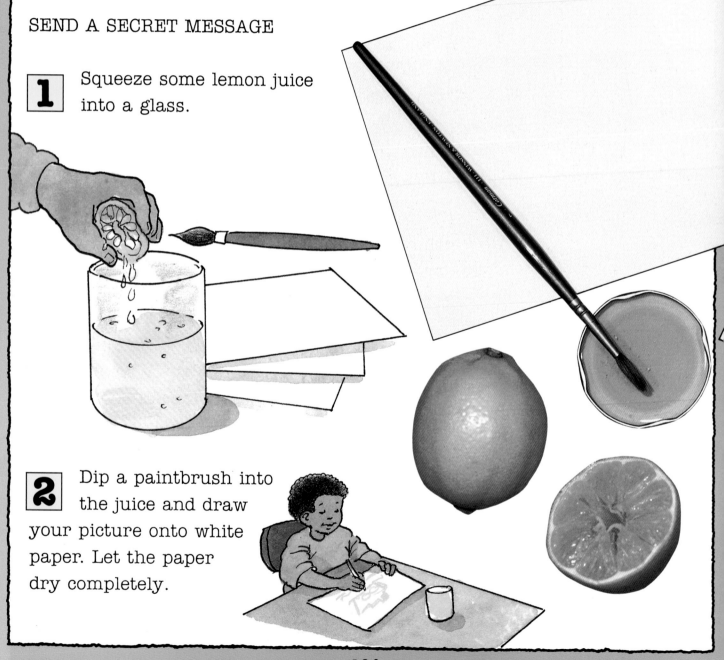

2 Dip a paintbrush into the juice and draw your picture onto white paper. Let the paper dry completely.

3 Ask an adult to place the paper in the oven for a few minutes, and the picture will reappear.

WHY IT WORKS

When the lemon juice is heated, water evaporates away. The compounds that remain combine with oxygen in the air. This turns the juice brown and makes the picture visible.

GET AN ADULT TO DO THIS

FURTHER IDEAS

Draw on white paper using a wax candle. Warm the paper on a radiator until the wax melts and the picture is revealed.

SPLITTING COLORS

If you look very carefully with a magnifying glass at the colored dots that make up the colors in this book, you may notice that there are only four colors. All of the other colors are made by mixing these colors together.

SEPARATE COLORED INKS

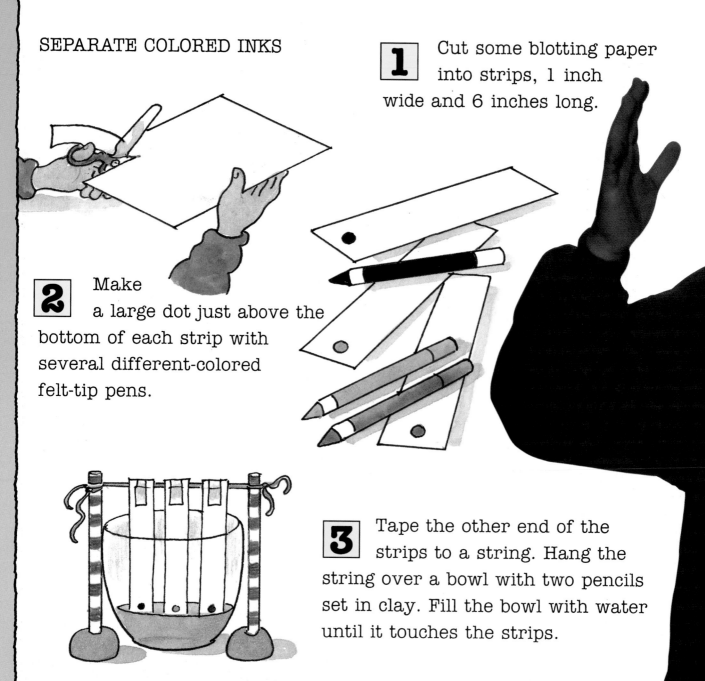

1 Cut some blotting paper into strips, 1 inch wide and 6 inches long.

2 Make a large dot just above the bottom of each strip with several different-colored felt-tip pens.

3 Tape the other end of the strips to a string. Hang the string over a bowl with two pencils set in clay. Fill the bowl with water until it touches the strips.

4 Watch the water rise half way up the strips. Remove them, and see how the colors have separated.

WHY IT WORKS

The inks are made from different colors. These are separated by the rising water because some travel through the paper faster than others. For example, green is made from blue and yellow.

FURTHER IDEAS
Mix some food coloring together. Repeat the experiment with one drop of this mixture and watch the coloring separate.

BURNING AND BREATHING

Air is really a mixture of many gases. Most of the air is made up of nitrogen. One fifth is made up of oxygen. Oxygen is needed for fires and for people to breathe. Without oxygen, fires wouldn't burn and people would suffocate and die.

INVESTIGATE A BURNING CANDLE

1 Use clay to stand a candle upright in the middle of a small, shallow saucer.

2 Place four piles of coins around the clay so that a jar can sit over the candle.

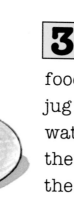

3 Add a few drops of food coloring to a jug filled with water. Then fill the saucer with the colored water.

WHY IT WORKS

The burning candle flame uses up the particles of oxygen. Water is sucked up into the jar to replace the used oxygen. Water rises about one fifth up the jar. The burning stops when all of the oxygen in the jar has been used up.

GET AN ADULT TO DO THIS

4 Ask an adult to light the candle and lower the jar over it. Watch the water level in the jar rise as the candle goes out.

FURTHER IDEAS
Compare how long similar candles burn when different jars are placed over them. The longer they burn, the more oxygen is present.

LIVING YEAST

Most germs, or "microbes," are bad for us, because they cause illness and disease. However, some microbes can be useful to us. We use microbes to make yogurt, cheese, bread, and beer. Yeast is a microbe that looks like a yellow powder, but under a microscope you can see that it is made of living cells.

SEE YEAST BREATHING

1 Find a glass bottle and pour in a teaspoonful of sugar and some dried yeast.

2 Pour in some warm water. Swirl the bottle to mix the water, sugar, and yeast.

3 Fit a balloon over the neck of the bottle and make sure it is sealed tightly.

4 Stand the bottle in a large bowl of hot water to keep it warm. Watch the mixture for bubbles of gas. Eventually, the balloon will fill with gas and inflate.

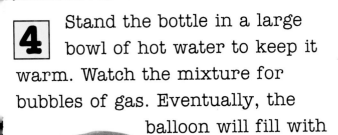

WHY IT WORKS

When you add the warm water, the yeast "wakes up" and feeds on the sugar. As it feeds, it breathes out carbon dioxide and fills the balloon.

FURTHER IDEAS

Stir a spoonful of sugar and dried yeast in warm water. Mix half a pound of flour with half an ounce of butter and a little salt. Add the yeast and water and knead into a dough. Bake the bread for fifteen minutes at 425°F (220°C).

CONTENTS

CHAPTER *Five*

UNDERSTANDING ELECTRICITY

WHAT IS ELECTRICITY?

All things are made up of tiny particles called atoms. Atoms are made from even smaller particles, some of which are electrically charged. This charge may be negative or positive. Electricity is a flow of the negatively-charged particles. You can see a flow of charge in the form of a spark.

LISTENING TO ELECTRICITY

1 Find a metal tray or a cookie tin lid. Place a lump of clay, large enough to use as a handle, in the middle of the tray.

2 Place the tray on a large plastic bag. Grip the clay firmly with one hand, press down, and rotate the tray vigorously for two minutes on the plastic.

3 Be very careful not to touch the tray with your hands. Lift the tray off the plastic with the clay grip.

4 Pick up a metal fork with your free hand. Touch the edge of the tray with it. Hear the sparks crackle!

WHY IT WORKS

As the tray is rubbed on the plastic, it becomes negatively-charged. The fork is positively-charged and when it is brought close to the tray it attracts the negative charges. They jump through the air to the fork as a spark.

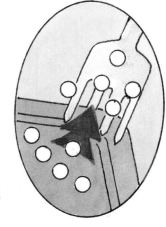

FURTHER IDEAS
Charge up a plastic comb by rubbing it vigorously on a clean, dry cloth. Adjust a faucet to give a thin stream of running water. Bring the comb close to the stream. The comb pulls at the water! Make the water dance by jiggling the comb.

STATIC ELECTRICITY

The ancient Greeks noticed that when amber (fossilized tree resin) is rubbed, it attracts light objects, such as feathers. This is because the amber has become electrically charged. The word *electricity* comes from the Greek word *elektron*, meaning amber. Scientists use an electroscope to check if an object is electrically charged.

MAKE AN ELECTROSCOPE

1 Find a clean jar. Cut a circle of cardboard big enough to fit over the top of a glass jar. Cut two ¹/₂ inch-long parallel slots in the middle of the cardboard.

2 Cut out two strips of aluminum foil. They should each be about ¹/₂ inch wide and 2 inches long.

3 Insert one strip through each slot so the strips overlap at the top. Tape the cardboard to the top of the jar so the strips hang downward.

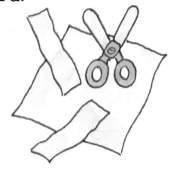

4 Charge up a plastic comb by rubbing it vigorously for a couple of minutes with a clean, dry cloth.

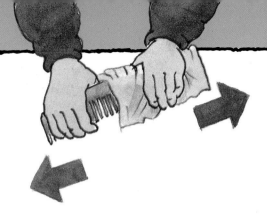

5 Test the comb for charge with your electroscope. Touch the top of the aluminum strips with the comb. Watch what happens to the two strips.

WHY IT WORKS

Electricity cannot move through plastic or amber. But they can hold a *static* (not moving) electric charge. When the comb touches the strips, the electric charge is released because electricity can move through metal.
Both strips receive the same kind of charge, and because like charges repel (push away) each other, the strips move apart.

FURTHER IDEAS
Inflate two balloons. Tie a piece of nylon thread to the end of each balloon. Rub each balloon on a wool sweater. Hang both balloons together from their threads. Watch how they repel each other.

BATTERY POWER

Static electricity is not very useful for powering machines, so we use *current* electricity. An electric current is a controlled flow of electric charge. Batteries produce electric currents from chemicals. Alessandro Volta made the first battery in 1800. The volt, a unit of electric measurement, is named after him.

MAKE A BATTERY

1 Find 12 copper coins and zinc washers of similar size. They will need to be stacked. Cut out 12 same-sized circles of blotting paper.

2 Pour vinegar into a glass with a tablespoonful of salt. Soak each piece of blotting paper in the mixture. Stack a coin, then a washer, on a piece of blotting paper. Finish with a washer.

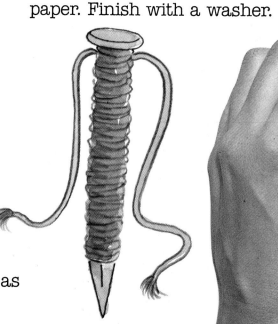

3 Take 6 ½ feet of thin plastic-coated copper wire. Coil it tightly around an iron nail as many times as you can.

4 Attach one end of the copper wire to the bottom coin and the other to the top washer.

WHY IT WORKS

The salt and vinegar start a chemical reaction. Negatively charged particles flow through the coins to the washers, around the wire coil, and back to the battery. The electric current creates a magnetic field that affects a compass needle (see pages 134-135).

5 Test your battery by bringing the nail close to a small compass. The nail should make the compass needle spin.

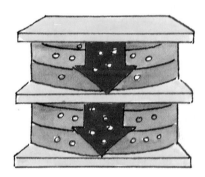

FURTHER IDEAS
Find a juicy lemon. Push one copper and one zinc nail into it. Touch both nails with your tongue. You will feel a tingle from the flow of current in the lemon "battery."

SIMPLE CIRCUITS

The path an electric current takes is called a circuit. Electric current flows from the power supply, to the lightbulb, and back to the power supply. As long as there are no gaps in the circuit, the electric current will flow.

MAKE A CIRCUIT

1 Ask an adult to open up a coat hanger. Bend it into a wavy shape. Push the ends of the wire into a cardboard base. Hold each end in place with clay.

2 Make a loop out of thin wire. Connect it to a long piece of insulated wire. Thread this through a plastic straw to form a handle. Slip the loop onto the wavy wire.

3 Attach a 6-volt lightbulb and 6-volt battery to the base. Wire the battery and bulb to the wavy wire as shown (right).

4 Connect the other end of the bulb to the loop. The wire needs to be long enough to reach both ends of the wavy wire.

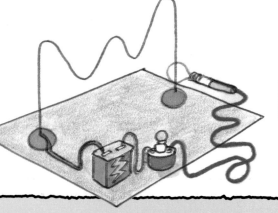

5 Check that the bulb lights when you touch the loop to the wavy wire. Now try and move the loop along the path of the wavy wire without letting the two touch!

WHY IT WORKS

Current electricity only flows if there is a complete circuit back to the battery. The gap in this circuit is between the loop and the wavy wire. The wires will touch if your hand is not steady. The gap is closed, the circuit is completed, and the bulb lights up.

FURTHER IDEAS

Try replacing the bulb in this circuit with a small electric buzzer. When you touch the wavy wire, the buzzer will buzz. You could make the game harder by making the wavy wire longer or even more wavy.

CONDUCTORS AND INSULATORS

Some materials allow electricity to flow through them easily. These materials are called electrical conductors. Most metals are good conductors. Other materials, like plastic, do not easily let electricity flow through them. These materials, called insulators, are used to prevent electricity from reaching places where it would be dangerous.

TEST FOR ELECTRICAL CONDUCTORS

1 Find a thick cardboard base. Cut out two squares of aluminum foil. Glue them onto the base. Leave a small gap between them (see right).

2 Attach a piece of thin plastic-coated copper wire to one square. Glue it to the board as shown. Repeat for the other square.

3 Connect one of the wires to a 6-volt lightbulb (right). Glue the bulb to the base.

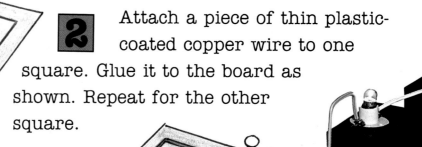

4 Connect the other wire to a 6-volt battery. Now connect the battery and bulb to a small plastic-coated copper wire.

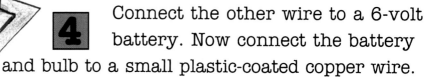

5 Test a range of objects, such as keys, pencils, or erasers by placing them across the two squares.

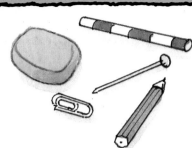

WHY IT WORKS

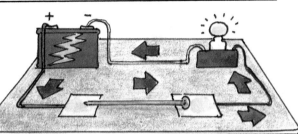

If an object is a conductor, it completes the circuit. The bulb lights up because conductors allow electricity to flow through them. All metals are conductors. Carbon is an unusual non-metal because it also conducts electricity. Pencil "lead" contains carbon in the form of graphite.

FURTHER IDEAS

Make up another circuit without a base. Test water to see if it can conduct electricity. Keep the squares close together in the container. Stir in lots of salt to help the water to conduct. Watch the bulb get brighter as you add more salt.

RESISTANCE

Good conductors of electricity allow electricity to flow easily. A thick wire can conduct more electricity than a thin wire, just like a wide road can carry more cars than a narrow road. The thin wire resists the flow of electricity or has a higher resistance.

MAKE A DIMMER SWITCH

1 Attach a 6-volt battery and 6-volt bulb to a thick cardboard base. Use two long wires and one short one to make a circuit as shown (right).

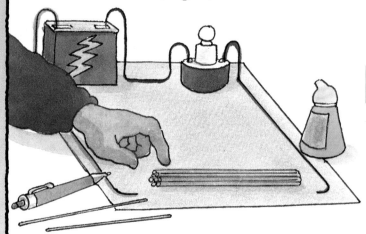

2 Remove the graphite from a mechanical pencil. Tape or glue together half a dozen graphite rods. Attach the wire from the battery to the bundle.

3 Attach a square of aluminum foil to the wire from the bulb. Check that the circuit is complete and the bulb lights when you touch the square to the graphite.

WHY IT WORKS

Graphite is made of carbon, which is a conductor. As you slide the square along the graphite toward the battery, the electricity travels less distance. This means less resistance, so the bulb gets brighter.

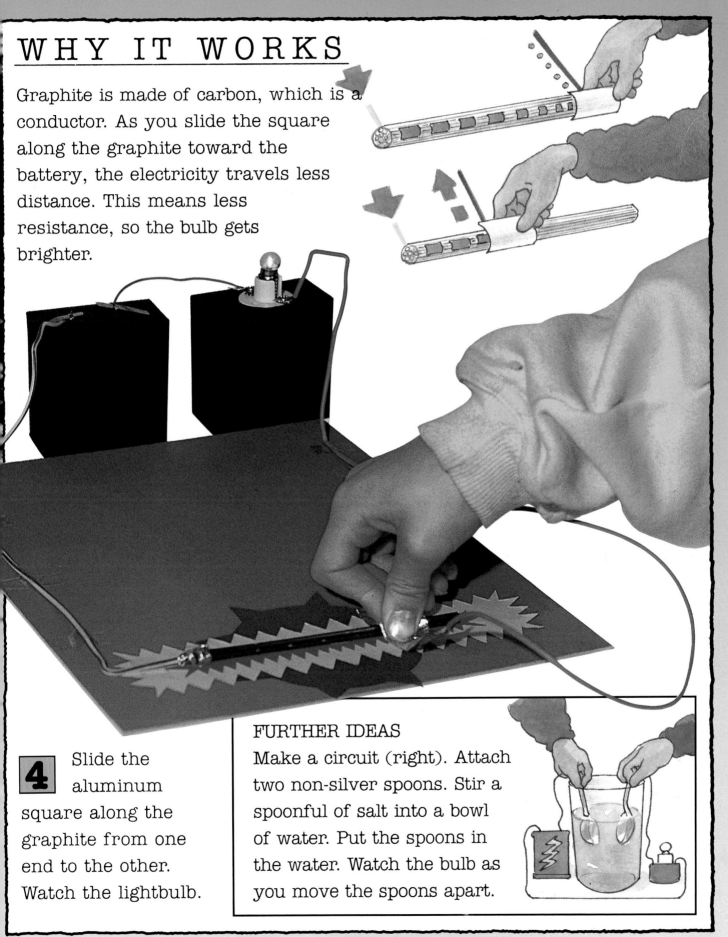

4 Slide the aluminum square along the graphite from one end to the other. Watch the lightbulb.

FURTHER IDEAS
Make a circuit (right). Attach two non-silver spoons. Stir a spoonful of salt into a bowl of water. Put the spoons in the water. Watch the bulb as you move the spoons apart.

OPEN CIRCUITS

Every time you turn on a light you are completing a circuit. As soon as a switch is closed (turned on), the circuit is completed and the electricity operates the bulb or electrical appliance. In 1837, Samuel Morse had the idea of completing and breaking an electrical circuit to send messages.

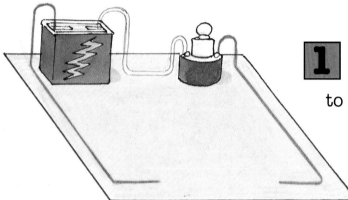

SEND A MESSAGE

1 Make a circuit using a 6-volt battery and 6-volt bulb attached to a thick cardboard base. Leave a gap between the two wires (see left).

2 Make a switch out of a steel paper clip. Attach it to the end of the wire running from the battery. Tape a square of aluminum foil over the top (see right). Tape another aluminum square over the end of the other wire. Make sure the paper clip reaches this square.

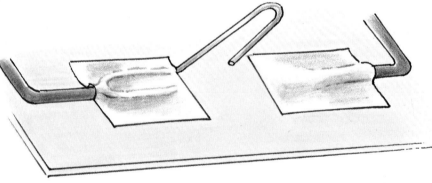

3 Press the paper clip down to touch the square and switch on the bulb. Practice long and short flashes to send a Morse code message.

WHY IT WORKS

Electricity cannot flow when a circuit is open. Closing the switch completes the circuit. The bulb lights immediately because electricity can travel so quickly.

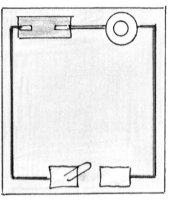

FURTHER IDEAS
Make a burglar alarm using your circuit board as a base. Tape some pencils or straws along the side edges. Place a second board on top of the pencils leaving the bulb and battery clear. Cover the boards with a mat. When the "intruder" steps on the mat, the switch will be pressed and the burglar alarm will light up.

TURNED ON

Being able to turn a light on or off from two different places can be very useful. If a light can be turned on or off from both the top and the bottom of a staircase then not only is it safer at night but energy is also saved. This kind of switch is called a two-way switch.

MAKE A TWO-WAY SWITCH

1 Fold a piece of cardboard into a wedge shape (shown right). Draw a line down the center. Stick down two pieces of cardboard on each side of the line and draw a staircase.

2 Make a circuit using a 6-volt battery and light-bulb. Push a tack through each piece of cardboard. Attach the wires to them.

3 Push four more tacks into the cardboard (shown below). Connect the upper two with a short piece of wire and repeat for the lower two.

4 Attach a paper clip under each of the first two tacks so that they can turn to touch either the upper or lower tack.

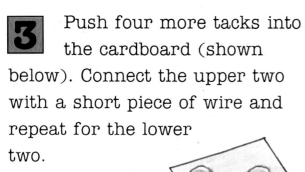

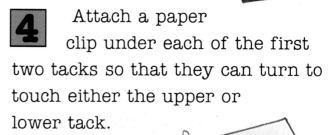

WHY IT WORKS

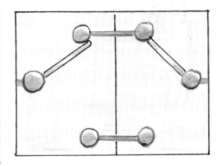
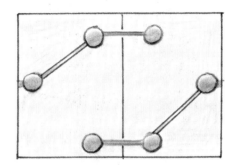
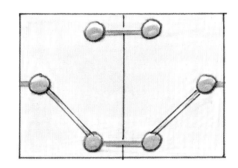

The two-way switch allows two alternative paths for an electric current. Electricity can flow only when both paper clips are touching the same wire. Removing one of the paper clips from the wire breaks the circuit.

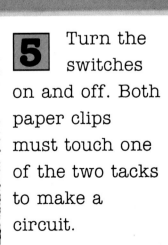

5 Turn the switches on and off. Both paper clips must touch one of the two tacks to make a circuit.

FURTHER IDEAS
Make a three-way switch quiz game (see right). When the paper clips point to the same letter, the bulb lights up. When your friend chooses the correct answer (A, B, or C), the bulb lights up.

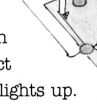

BIGGER CIRCUITS

All the circuits you have built so far have been small and simple, requiring only one piece of wire. Electric circuits in your home consist of many more wires. Finding which wire is connected to which source can be like finding your way through a maze.

MAKE A MAZE

1 Find a large piece of thick cardboard. Cut out ½ inch-wide strips of aluminum foil about the same length as the cardboard.

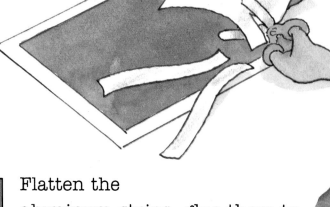

2 Flatten the aluminum strips, glue them to the cardboard, then make a crisscross pattern with the strips.

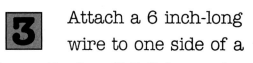

3 Attach a 6 inch-long wire to one side of a 6-volt lightbulb. Then attach a 3.5 ft-long wire to a dowel "pointer," leaving the copper exposed at the end.

4 Make a circuit (left). Wire the battery to the aluminum at one corner of the board. Test the circuit by touching the pointer to the foil.

5 Cover parts of the aluminum with insulating tape. Copy the pattern shown at the bottom of the page. The gray shaded areas show where the tape should go.

6 Challenge a friend to find a way through the maze keeping the bulb lit. The pointer must touch only the aluminum to complete the circuit.

WHY IT WORKS

When the pointer touches any part of the aluminum connected to the battery, a circuit is created. Electricity can flow and light the bulb. If the pointer touches other parts of the maze, the bulb goes out.

HOUSE LIGHTS

A simple way to arrange more than one lightbulb is in a series, so the electricity flows through one bulb to the next. But if a bulb fails, the circuit is broken, and all the lights go out. In a parallel circuit, each bulb has its own connection to the battery, so if one bulb fails the others are unaffected. House lights work this way.

MAKE A RING CIRCUIT

1 Ask an adult to bend two pieces of wire into two rings, one larger than the other. Use some cardboard as a base for your circuit.

2 Make a circuit out of the two rings and a 6-volt battery (left). Connect the outer ring to one battery terminal, and the inner ring to the other terminal.

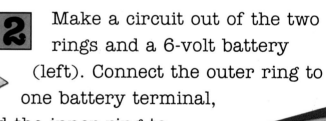

3 Connect two pieces of thin plastic-coated copper wire to the ends of a 6-volt bulb. Check that there is plenty of bare wire showing at the free ends.

WHY IT WORKS

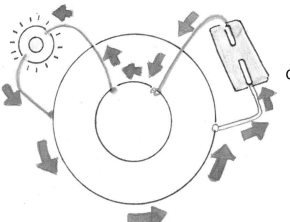

Wherever the battery and bulb are placed on the rings, there is always a complete circuit. This type of parallel circuit is called a ring circuit.

4 Attach one of the wires running from the lightbulb to the outer ring, and one to the inner ring. It forms a circuit and the bulb lights up.

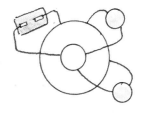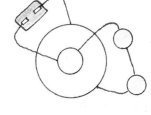

FURTHER IDEAS
Try adding another bulb to your ring circuit. Does one affect the other? Can you find a place on the rings where the circuit does not work?

MOVEMENT FROM ELECTRICITY

Electric motors do all sorts of useful work in the home: They are found in household items such as washing machines, electric heaters, and food processors. The movement produced is usually a spinning motion. The electric motor uses electricity and magnetism to produce movement.

MAKE A SIMPLE MOTOR

1 Wrap four 3.5-foot pieces of wire together to form a loop (see right). Secure the wires with insulation tape.

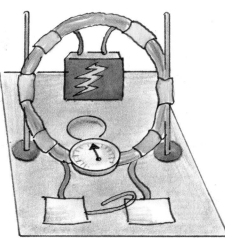

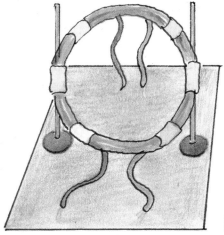
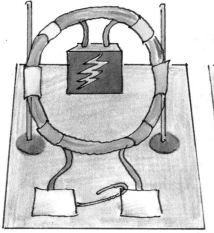

2 On a cardboard base, attach two dowels in an upright position with clay. Tape the wire to the dowels (shown above).

3 Attach the two top wires to a 6-volt battery. Attach the bottom wires to two aluminum squares at the base. Make a switch out of a paper clip.

4 Leave the switch open. Hold a small pocket compass level in the middle of the wire loop. Note the direction the compass points to.

5 Now turn off the switch and watch the effect on the compass. It should spin around until you turn the switch on again.

WHY IT WORKS

Electric current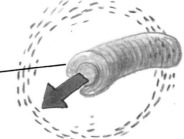

Magnetic field

When electricity flows through a wire it creates a magnetic field. When another magnet (the pointer in a compass) is close, the magnets push or pull each other.

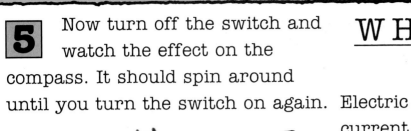

FURTHER IDEAS
Coil about three and a half feet of copper wire around an iron nail. Attach the ends of the wire to the terminals of a 6-volt battery. The nail will become an electromagnet which is strong enough to attract steel paper clips.

ELECTROPLATING

An electric current can be used to split chemicals into the elements that they are made of. If an electric current is passed through a liquid called an electrolyte, charged particles will move through it. This is called electrolysis. Cutlery and jewelry are silverplated using electrolysis.

COPPERPLATE A SILVER COIN

1 Fill a clean glass jar with water. This will act as your electrolyte.

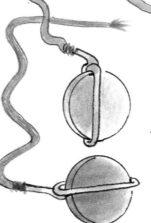

2 Find a copper coin and a silver coin. Wrap the bare copper ends of two pieces of long, thin wire around each coin (see left).

3 Put the coins into the water. Wrap the two wires around a pencil balanced over the top of the jar.

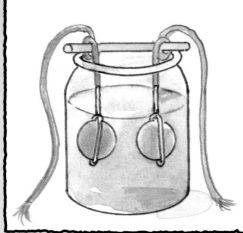

4 Connect the copper coin to the positive (+) terminal of a 6-volt battery, and the silver coin to the negative (-) terminal.

5 Make sure the coins are close but not touching. Leave the circuit set up for five minutes.

Take out the two coins and observe.

WHY IT WORKS

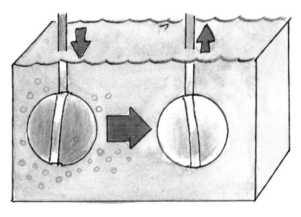

Electric current enters the water through the positive terminal attached to the copper coin. It carries some of the copper with it. The current carries the copper through the water to the silver coin. The copper is left as a thin layer over the silver coin. The copper can easily be scraped off afterward. Dispose of the water carefully because it is poisonous.

FURTHER IDEAS

Try using vinegar with lots of salt stirred into it as the electrolyte instead of water. Using a more powerful battery produces faster and thicker plating.

CONTENTS

CHAPTER *Six*

MAKING THINGS FLOAT AND SINK

WHY DO THINGS FLOAT?

Wood, cork and ice all float no matter what size or shape they are. However, materials such as modeling clay or steel, sometimes float and sometimes sink. With these materials, it is their shape that decides whether they float or sink.

MAKE A CLAY BOAT

1 Fill a large plastic bowl with water from the tap.

2 Try to float a lump of modeling clay on the surface of the water. Try floating marbles too. Watch them sink.

3 Using your thumbs, press the clay into a boat shape. Hollow out the inside.

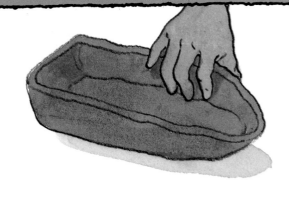

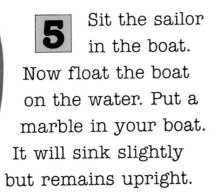

4 Draw a sailor on a sheet of cardboard. Color him in and cut out. Fold along the dotted lines as shown so he can sit up.

5 Sit the sailor in the boat. Now float the boat on the water. Put a marble in your boat. It will sink slightly but remains upright.

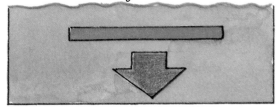

Clay sinks

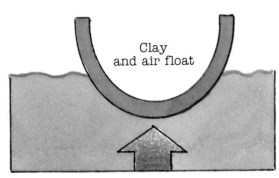

Clay and air float

FURTHER IDEAS
Have a boat-building competition with some friends. Each make a boat using the same amount of clay. Whose boat can hold the most marbles?

WHY IT WORKS

One ounce of water takes up more space than one ounce of clay. Because clay is denser than water it sinks. Shaped into a boat, clay fills with air. Air and clays together are less dense than water, so the boat floats.

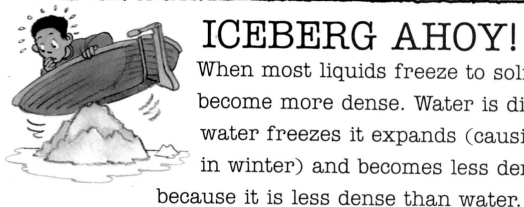

ICEBERG AHOY!

When most liquids freeze to solids they become more dense. Water is different. When water freezes it expands (causing burst pipes in winter) and becomes less dense. Ice floats because it is less dense than water.

Giant blocks of ice floating in the sea are called icebergs. Ships must take care to avoid icebergs.

WATCH AN ICE-CUBE MELT

1 Add some food coloring to a jar of water. Add enough coloring to turn the water a bright color.

2 Pour the colored water into an ice-cube tray. Put it in a freezer overnight.

3 Fill up a large container with hot tap water. Ask an adult to help you.

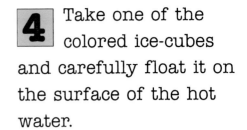

4 Take one of the colored ice-cubes and carefully float it on the surface of the hot water.

5 As the ice becomes water, the color moves around in the warmer water. It sinks to the bottom of the container.

WHY IT WORKS

As the ice melts to water its density increases. This makes it sink to the bottom of the container. There it mixes with the water in the jar and warms up. It becomes less dense and moves back toward the surface.

Melted ice

FURTHER IDEAS
Make a volcano. Fill a jar with hot water. Add coloring. Cover the top of the jar with paper held in place with a rubber band. Put the jar in a bowl of cold water. Pierce the paper. Watch the volcano erupt.

COLORFUL PAPER

It is not only boats and icebergs that float on water. Oil-based liquids that are less dense than water also float on top of water. We sometimes see escaped crude oil floating on the sea in a thin layer that stretches for miles. Such oil slicks can harm the seabed, fish, and birds.

MAKE COLORED PAPER

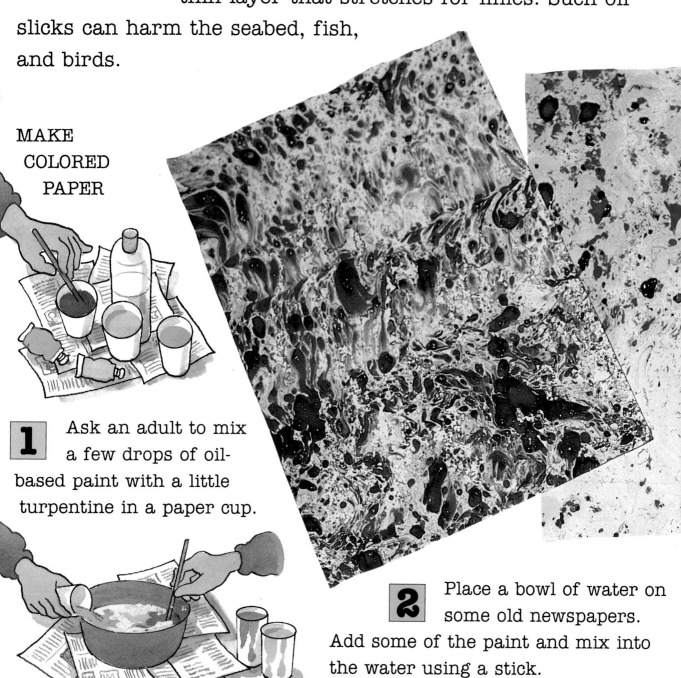

1 Ask an adult to mix a few drops of oil-based paint with a little turpentine in a paper cup.

2 Place a bowl of water on some old newspapers. Add some of the paint and mix into the water using a stick.

3 Carefully lower a sheet of plain paper onto the surface of the water. Let the paper soak up the paint.

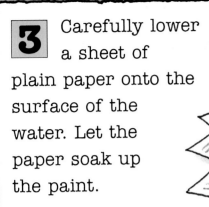

WHY IT WORKS

Oil paints are less dense than water so they float on the surface. For this reason salad oil floats on top of vinegar. You can make the separate layers mix together by shaking them hard.

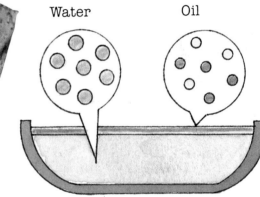

Water   Oil

4 Remove the paper and leave it to dry. Repeat using fresh paper. Stir the water to get different patterns.

FURTHER IDEAS

Try making different patterns by changing the colors of paint. Let the papers dry. Use your favorite patterns for writing paper.

FLOATING LIQUIDS

Many liquids are like water and mix easily with it. But some liquids do not mix with water unless they are forced to. Oils and syrups do not mix well with water. Some liquids are less dense and float on top of water (see pages 144-145). Others are denser so water floats on top of them.

GET AN ADULT TO DO THIS FOR YOU

MAKE LAYERS OF FLOATING LIQUIDS

1 Find a clean, empty plastic soda bottle. Ask an adult to cut the top off with a sharp knife.

2 Slowly pour in some syrup so there is a ³/₄ inch layer in the bottom. Let the syrup settle.

3 Next, slowly pour ³/₄ inch of cooking oil over the layer of syrup.

4 Finally, carefully pour in about ³/₄ inch of water.

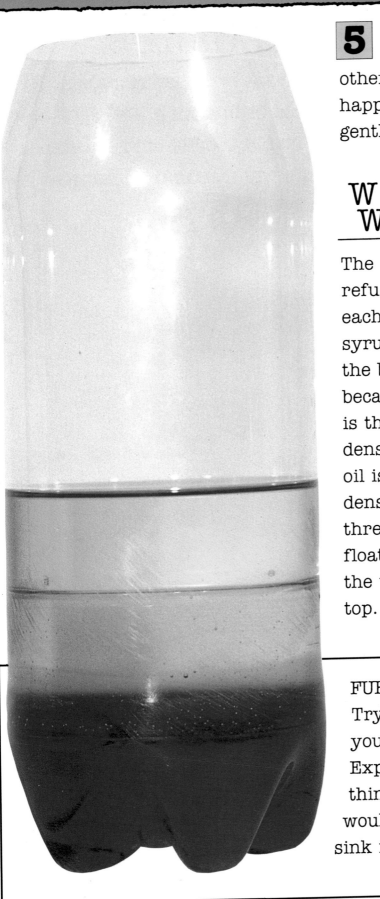

5 Examine the three layers. They float on top of each other without mixing. See what happens if you stir gently with a spoon.

WHY IT WORKS

The layers of liquid refuse to mix with each other. The syrup is at the bottom because it is the densest. The oil is the least dense of the three and so floats on the very top.

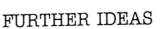

FURTHER IDEAS
Try floating different objects on your layers of liquid. Experiment with things that you would expect to sink in water.

FLOATING EGGS

How can you tell whether an egg is good or bad without breaking it? Fresh eggs sink if placed in a bowl of fresh water because they are denser than water. But if an egg turns bad, it floats in water. This is because the yolk and white have dried up, which makes it less dense than a good egg.

MAKE AN EGG FLOAT

GET AN ADULT TO DO THIS FOR YOU

1 Find two large containers. Fill one with hot tap water and the other with cold tap water. Get an adult to help.

2 Add a spoonful of table salt to the hot water. Stir in the salt until it has all dissolved.

3 Put a fresh egg into the salty water to see if it floats. If it doesn't, add more salt until it does.

WHY IT WORKS

Salt dissolved in water increases the density of water. Denser liquids are better at keeping objects afloat.

This is why many things that sink in fresh water will float in salted water.

4 You cannot float the egg in fresh water but in salty water the same egg floats. Challenge your friends to explain it!

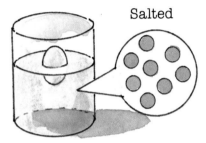

Salted

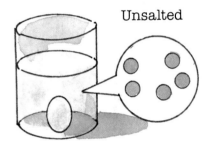

Unsalted

FURTHER IDEAS

See how long it takes for a fresh egg to go bad when not refrigerated. Test it in a vase of fresh water each day. Dispose of the bad egg *carefully* when you've finished.

DIFFERENT DEPTHS

We have seen that each liquid has its own particular density. The denser or "heavier" the liquid, the better it is at making things float in it. Brewers of beer need to know the exact density of beer to ensure the beer tastes just right. A hydrometer is used to test its density.

MAKE A HYDROMETER

1 Pour equal amounts of syrup, cooking oil and hot water into three containers of the same size.

2 Cut a plastic drinking straw into three equal lengths. Each will make a hydrometer.

3 Make three small balls out of clay. Attach one to the end of each straw.

FURTHER IDEAS

Float your hydrometer in a bowl of water. Add salt or sugar to the water. What effect does this have on the hydrometer?

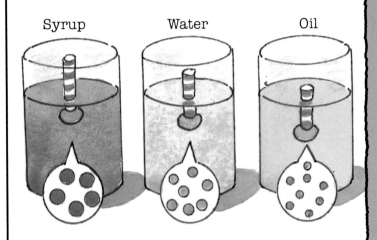

WHY IT WORKS

Syrup   Water   Oil

The particles of dense liquids are bigger or closer together. Dense liquids push harder on the hydrometer. The harder the push, the higher up in the liquid the hydrometer floats.

4 Carefully place each hydrometer into the liquids. Compare the different levels at which the hydrometers float.

UNSINKABLE

Boats and ships are always built to be as stable as possible. This means that they do not get pushed over easily by waves in rough seas. Most boats and ships capsize and sink if they are pushed too far. A buoy is a channel marker. Because it is there to warn of danger, it is vital that it never gets pushed over.

MAKE A BUOY

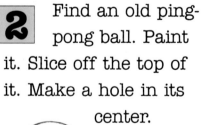

1 Half fill a large container with water.

2 Find an old ping-pong ball. Paint it. Slice off the top of it. Make a hole in its center.

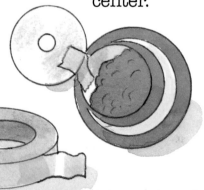

GET AN ADULT TO DO THIS FOR YOU

3 Fill the inside of the buoy with clay and tape the top back on.

4 Make a flag out of a triangle of paper and a drinking straw.

5 Stick the flag into the hole in the top of the buoy.

6 Put the buoy in the water. Make some waves. See how difficult it is to push the buoy over.

WHY IT WORKS

The clay acts as "ballast." Ballast is spare weight. The ballast pulls downward into the water and keeps the buoy upright. Boats carry ballast to keep them stable at sea.

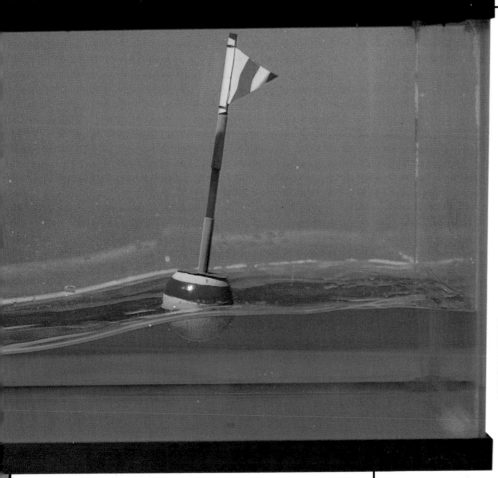

FURTHER IDEAS
Compare the stability of your buoy with the boat you made on page 141. Waves lapping over the side of the boat can easily cause it to capsize.

PORT AND STARBOARD

You may have noticed that ships and large boats have steering wheels. Smaller boats have a tiller instead. Both wheel and tiller are used to control a "rudder." The rudder is used to steer the boat.

At sea, sailors say "port" for left and "starboard" for right.

MAKE A BOAT WITH A RUDDER

GET AN ADULT TO HELP YOU WITH THIS

1 Ask an adult to cut a boat shape from a piece of styrofoam. Make two holes as shown.

2 Make a brightly colored sail out of thin paper. Push a wooden stick through the sail.

3 Push the stick into the hole at the pointed end of the boat. Hold in place with clay.

4 Cut a rudder out of a waterproof milk carton. Tape it to a drinking straw.

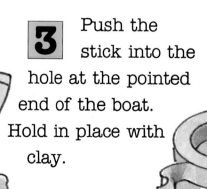

Cocktail sticks

Rudder

5 Push the straw through the other hole. Hold the straw in place by pushing two cut-off cocktail sticks through it.

6 Launch the boat, blow into the sail and steer by turning the rudder.

WHY IT WORKS

1   2   3

If the rudder points in line with the flow of water (2) the boat moves straight on. If the rudder points to the left or right (1, 3), the flow of water is slowed by it and so the boat changes direction.

FURTHER IDEAS
Try to adjust the rudder of your boat so that the boat sails around in a circle when you blow into the sail.

JET POWER

Most boats and ships have propellers which push them along. The propeller cuts through the water, pushing it back behind the vessel. This push against the water "propels", or makes the vessel move forward. A jet-propelled boat can travel at high speeds without a propeller. The "jet", or fast-moving flow of water, pushes the boat along.

MAKE A JET BOAT

1 Decorate an old plastic soda bottle. Weight the bottom of the bottle with clay.

2 Ask an adult to make a hole near the bottom of the bottle (right).

3 Place a balloon inside the bottle. Make sure you do not drop the balloon.

4 Stretch the balloon neck over the tap. Fill the balloon half full with water.

5 Pinch the balloon neck closed. Put clay around the bottle neck to weight the bottle.

6 Still holding the end of the balloon, put the bottle in the bath.

7 Let go of the balloon. Watch the jet of water shoot out and push the boat along.

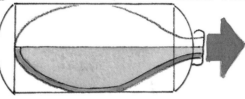

WHY IT WORKS

Boat moves forward   Water out

When the water shoots out of the balloon, it pushes against the water in the bath. This pushing force propels the jet boat forward. The quicker the water escapes from the balloon, the faster the boat travels.

FURTHER IDEAS

Cut a boat shape out of cardboard. Make a hole near the stern of the boat. Cut from the stern of the boat to the hole. Float the boat. Drop liquid soap in the hole. The boat will shoot forward.

DIVE DEEP!

Deep under the oceans are some of the last unexplored places on Earth. Deep-sea divers use vessels which can sink to the bottom and then float back to the surface again. Some marine animals such as jellyfish are also able to dive to great depths, then surface again.

MAKE A DIVING JELLYFISH

1 Find a large, clean plastic soda bottle. Fill it up to the top with tap water.

2 Cut both ends off a flexible plastic drinking straw to make a "U" shape.

3 Unbend a paper clip. Bend it into shape (shown at right). Push it into the ends of the straw.

WHY IT WORKS

When you squeeze the bottle, water is pushed into the straw, compressing the air. Water weighs more than air so the jellyfish gets heavier and sinks.

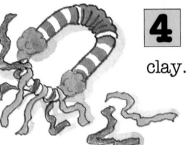

4 Roll out three thin strips of clay. Loop them around the paper clip.

5 This is your jellyfish. Drop it into the bottle and screw the top back on. To make the jellyfish dive, squeeze the bottle.

FURTHER IDEAS
Try making a diver from a small eye-dropper. Fill the dropper almost to the top with water then put it into the bottle of water.

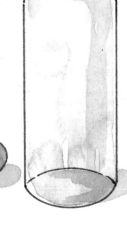

FLOATING UNDERWATER

Submarines are special floating vessels because they can sink and then return to the surface. Ballast tanks control how deep they dive. To make the submarine sink, the tanks are filled with water. To make the submarine rise, the water is pumped out and replaced with air.

FLOATING UNDERWATER

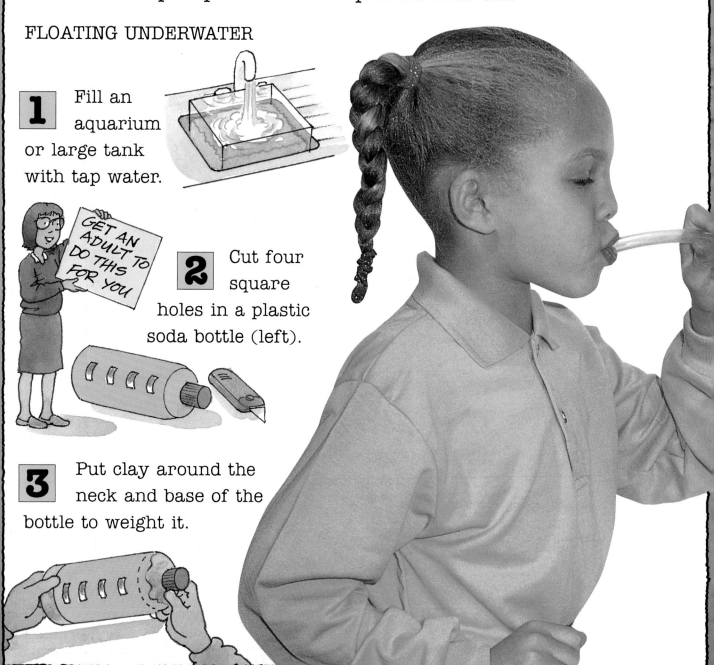

1 Fill an aquarium or large tank with tap water.

GET AN ADULT TO DO THIS FOR YOU

2 Cut four square holes in a plastic soda bottle (left).

3 Put clay around the neck and base of the bottle to weight it.

4 On the other side of the bottle make three holes. Make one large enough to fit a plastic tube.

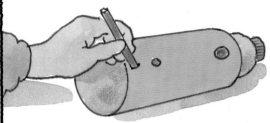

5 Decorate your submarine. Push the end of the tube into the larger of the three holes.

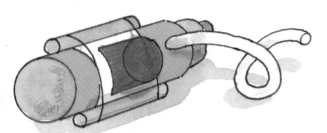

6 Try out your submarine. It will fill with water and sink. Blow into the tube to make it rise.

WHY IT WORKS

The submarine sinks when it fills with water (ballast). When you blow into the tube, the water is forced out and replaced by the air. Air is less dense than water so the submarine surfaces.

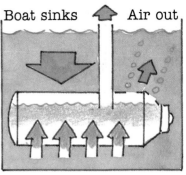

Boat sinks   Air out

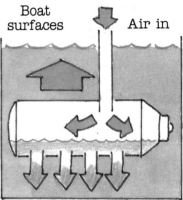

Boat surfaces   Air in

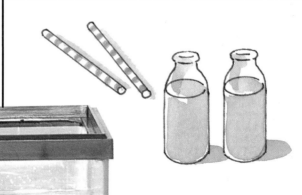

FURTHER IDEAS
Put an empty bottle in the bottom of your aquarium. Let it fill with water. Now blow air into it with a straw to make the bottle rise.

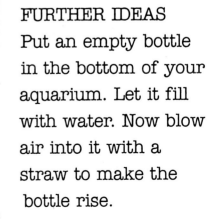

FLOATING ON AIR

The hovercraft is one of the great inventions of the twentieth century. It can travel on water or on land. The engines suck in air and then pump it downward. This creates a cushion of air that keeps the hovercraft from touching the surface over which it is traveling. The passengers enjoy a smooth and bump-free journey.

GET AN ADULT TO DO THIS FOR YOU

MAKE A HOVERCRAFT

1 Ask an adult to cut the top off a plastic soda bottle for you.

2 Wrap some clay around the base of the cut-off bottle top.

3 Make a skirt of paper to go around the clay. Make sure it hangs over it.

4 Blow up a balloon. Pinch the end. Carefully wrap the balloon around the bottle neck without letting it deflate.

5 Find a smooth surface. Place the hovercraft on it and let go of the balloon. Watch your hovercraft glide along.

WHY IT WORKS

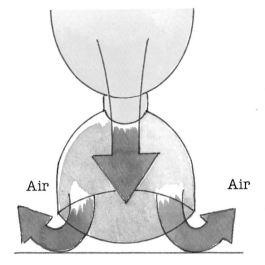

Air   Air

Air from the balloon escapes into the bottle top. The air pressure builds up until it creates a cushion that lifts the bottle slightly. It is the downward force of air that makes the hovercraft hover.

FURTHER IDEAS

Cut a hole in the bottom of a plastic margarine tub. Turn it upside down and fill it with air from a hairdrier. Watch it hover. Fill a paper bag with hot air from a hairdrier. What happens?

CONTENTS

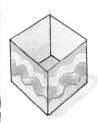

CHAPTER *Seven*

PLAYING WITH MAGNETS

WHAT IS A MAGNET?

People have known about magnets for thousands of years. The first magnets were made out of black rocks called lodestones which are found naturally in the ground. Some metal objects are attracted to this rock. Modern magnets are made from steel. They can be made into almost any shape – horseshoe, bar or ring.

MAKE A FISHING GAME

1 Draw some fish shapes on thin cardboard. Color them in and cut them out. Attach a steel paper clip to each fish.

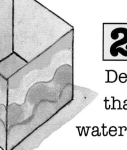

2 Find a large, clean cardboard box. Decorate the outside so that it looks like the water in a pond.

3 Make two fishing rods. Tie a 30 inch-long piece of string to each stick. Tape a magnet to the end of the string.

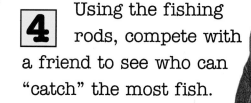

4 Using the fishing rods, compete with a friend to see who can "catch" the most fish.

WHY IT WORKS

Magnet — Force

Magnets "attract" some metals, meaning they pull some metals toward them. This pull is called magnetic force. You can feel this force when you pull the paper clip off the magnet.

We call objects that are attracted to magnets, magnetic.

FURTHER IDEAS

Collect together any objects you think may be magnetic. Try objects such as nails, screws, knitting needles, pins and aluminum foil. Make a list of the objects that are attracted to your magnet.

LONG-RANGE FORCE

How far away can the magnetic force work? Scientists use magnets that will attract objects from many feet away. Your magnet can attract objects a few inches away. When a magnet and object touch, they "stick" together as if fixed with glue.

MAKE A FLYING BUTTERFLY

1 Find a clean cardboard box. Ask an adult to cut away two opposite sides leaving a "U" shape (shown right).

GET AN ADULT TO HELP YOU WITH THIS

2 Tape a strong bar-shaped magnet along one side of the box (see left).

3 On thin paper, draw and cut out a butterfly shape. Push a thumbtack into one wing (see right). Tie a length of thread to the tack.

4 Tape the loose end of the thread to the side of the box opposite the magnet. When the thread is pulled taut, the butterfly should almost touch the magnet.

5 Stand the box up so the magnet is at the top. Hold the butterfly just below the magnet and let it float. Adjust the length of the thread to get the best floating effect.

WHY IT WORKS

Magnet's pull

Gravity's pull

The magnet is strong enough to attract the thumbtack from about an inch away. The magnetic pull on the thumbtack is strong enough to overcome the force of gravity trying to pull the tack to the ground. This leaves the butterfly floating in mid-air.

FURTHER IDEAS
Make a boat out of cork. Push a thumbtack into one end and then attach a paper sail. Float it in a bowl of water. Now hold a magnet close to the boat and see if it moves.

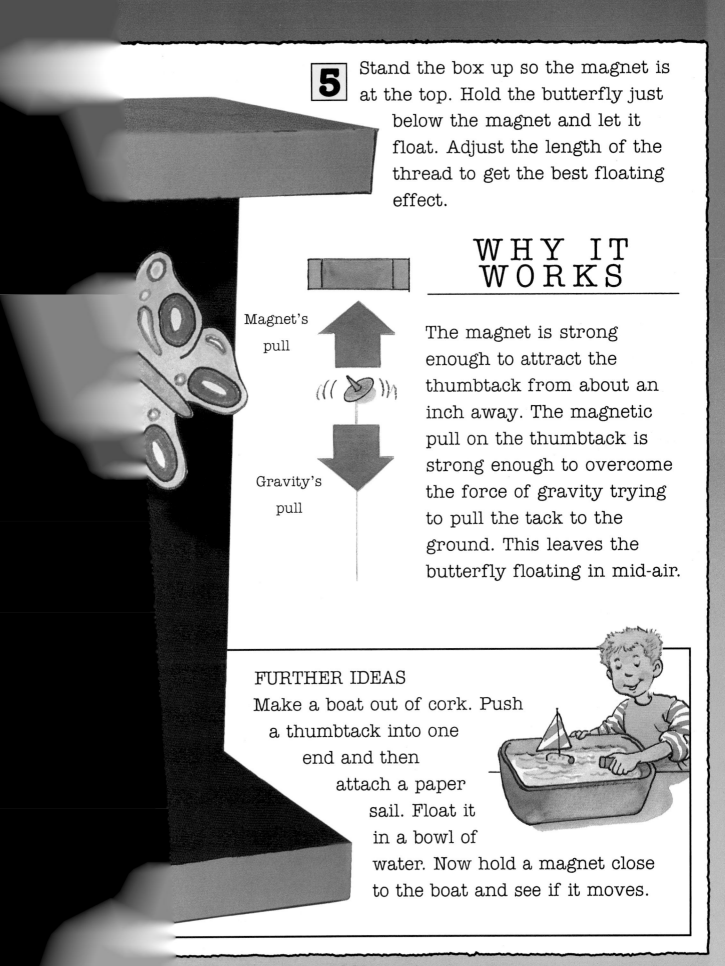

THROUGH AND THROUGH

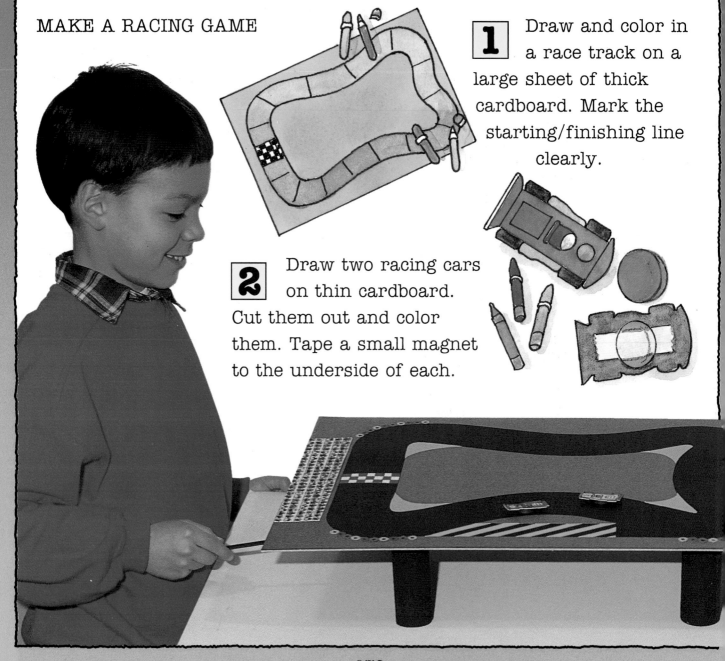

You can stick paper notes to the metal door of a refrigerator with a magnet. The paper and paint cannot block the magnetic force. If the magnetism is strong enough it can work straight through materials as if they were not there. This can be useful for making things move without touching them.

MAKE A RACING GAME

1 Draw and color in a race track on a large sheet of thick cardboard. Mark the starting/finishing line clearly.

2 Draw two racing cars on thin cardboard. Cut them out and color them. Tape a small magnet to the underside of each.

3 Find four cardboard tubes of the same size. Place one under each corner of the race track so it is raised.

4 Find two long, thin sticks. Tape a small magnet to one end of each.

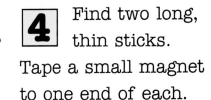

5 You can move your car with the magnet from underneath the race track. Race against a friend, taking care not to mix up each other's cars!

WHY IT WORKS

The magnets under the car and on the stick are attracted to each other. The magnetic force goes through the race track, although the race track does slightly weaken the force.

FURTHER IDEAS
Without getting your fingers wet, try to remove a steel paper clip from a glass of water. Move your magnet along the outside of the glass.

CHAIN REACTION

You may have noticed that when magnetic metals touch a magnet they will attract magnetic metals too. We can use this characteristic to build a "chain" of magnetic objects outward from a permanent magnet. Permanent magnets stay magnetic unless they are dropped or get too hot.

MAKE A MAGNETIC SCULPTURE

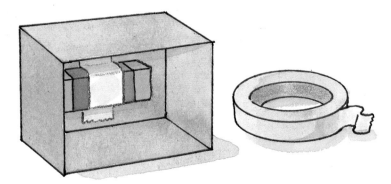

1 Find a small cardboard box. Tape a small magnet to the inside of the bottom of the box. Turn the box upside down.

2 Decorate the box with your own pattern and color it with bright colors.

3 Place a few steel paper clips on top of the box above the magnet. Build up a sculpture by adding pins, tacks and nails.

4 Change the shape until you are satisfied with your sculpture. You can reshape it endlessly.

WHY IT WORKS

When a magnetic metal is attracted to a permanent magnet it becomes a magnet too. It can attract other objects but only while it is touching a permanent magnet. This is called "induced" magnetism.

FURTHER IDEAS
Hang a magnet over the edge of a box and tape it into place. Try to form a chain by hanging paper clips from the end of the magnet.

MAGNETIC METALS

There are many different metals, but only three pure metals can be magnetized. These are iron, nickel and cobalt. None of the other pure metals – gold, silver, aluminum – can be made into magnets. But if you mix pure metals together their magnetic characteristics can be altered.

MAKE A COIN TESTER

1 Ask an adult to cut a slot at one end of a shoe box (see right). The slot should be just bigger than your largest coin.

GET AN ADULT TO HELP YOU WITH THIS

2 Cut out a strip of cardboard. Fold into an "L" shape. Tape into place just to the left of the slot.

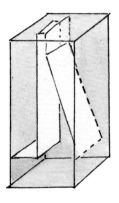

3 Cut another strip of cardboard, creasing it ³/₄ inch from the top. Tape this end to the right of the slot. Tape the other end to the side of the box.

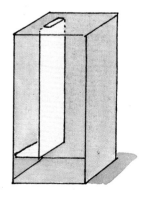

4 Cut another strip of cardboard. Fold into the shape shown (right). Make sure it fits into the triangular space between the first pieces.

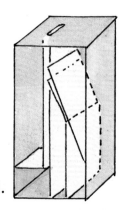

5 Find a strong magnet. Tape it inside the box just to the right of the slot.

6 Drop your coins into the slot. Most will fall to the left side of the box. If you drop iron or steel washers into the slot they will fall to the right side of the box.

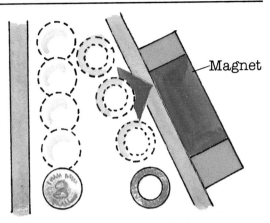

Magnet

Most coins are made from non-magnetic metals such as a copper mix. When you drop them into the box they are not attracted to the magnet and so fall straight down. When you drop iron or steel objects they are attracted by the magnet and are pulled over to the right side of the box.

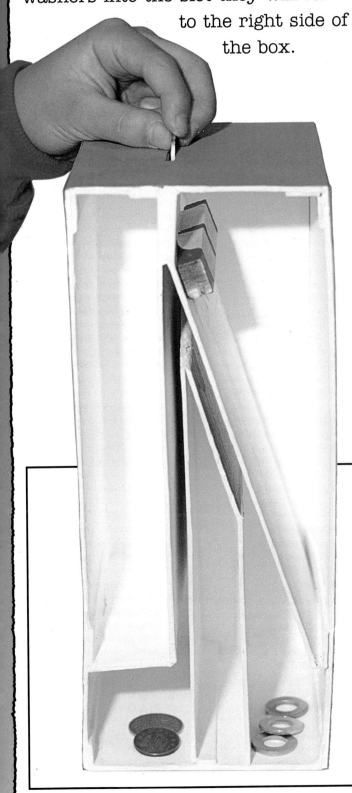

FURTHER IDEAS

Tableware is often made of stainless steel. Make a ramp out of cardboard and roll spoons or forks down it. Put a magnet under the ramp. See how it affects the path of the tableware. Why not try toy cars as well?

PUSH AND PULL

Magnets have two points where their power is strongest. These are called poles. Every magnet has a north and a south pole. When iron or steel touches a permanent magnet it has poles too (pages 172-173). A good way of testing whether an object is a permanent magnet or not is to see if it will "repel", or push away, another magnet.

MAKE A MAGNET FLOAT

1 Find a cardboard box. Ask an adult to cut away the sides and the middle of the box to leave the shape (shown at right).

GET AN ADULT TO HELP YOU WITH THIS

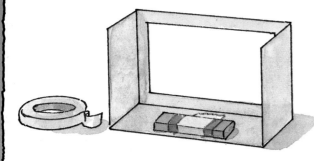

2 Tape down a strong bar magnet to the base of the box (left).

3 Copy the shape (shown at right) onto a piece of cardboard and cut out. Tape an identical magnet to the cardboard. Fold the cardboard around the magnet.

4 Hold the second magnet on top of the first with both north and south poles facing the same way, tape them together.

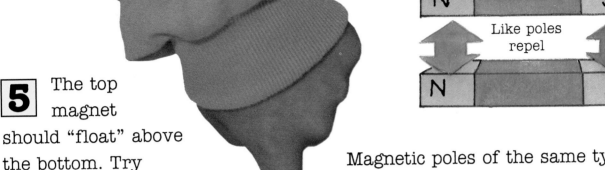

N ··· S

Like poles repel

N ··· S

5 The top magnet should "float" above the bottom. Try pushing the top magnet.

Magnetic poles of the same type repel each other. Gravity is trying to pull the top magnet down, but the two magnets are repelling each other with such force that the top one is held above the bottom. The top magnet would spring away if it wasn't taped in place.

FURTHER IDEAS

Find three horseshoe-shaped magnets. Thread them onto two pencils (shown at right). Line up the poles. See if you can make the magnets float. Try doing the same thing with ring-shaped magnets. Which works best?

USEFUL MAGNETS

Doctors have used magnets to pull tiny bits of iron out of a patient's eye. The advantage of using a magnet is that nothing needs to touch the injured eye. The magnet's ability to attract some materials but not others has been used in many ways. Giant magnets are used to sort out different waste metals.

MAKE A TREASURE HUNT

1 Make a desert island by filling a bowl almost to the top with clean, dry sand.

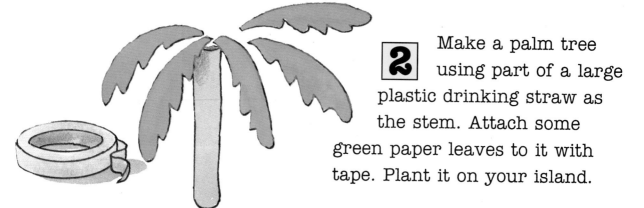

2 Make a palm tree using part of a large plastic drinking straw as the stem. Attach some green paper leaves to it with tape. Plant it on your island.

3 Make a treasure chest out of colored cardboard. Now find some treasure to put in it. An iron or steel bolt will do.

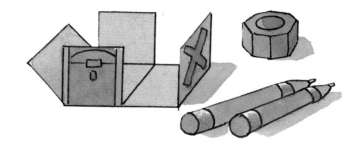

4 Bury the treasure chest in the sand. Make sure it is fairly near to the surface.

5 Search for the treasure using a magnet. You can take turns with a friend to find it.

WHY IT WORKS

You can hunt for the treasure by moving the magnet over the surface of the sand. When you hold the magnet directly over the steel treasure, the magnet strongly attracts it. The magnetic force goes straight through the sand.

FURTHER IDEAS
Sort out aluminum soda cans that can be recycled by testing each can with a magnet. Aluminum cans are not magnetic.

VERY ATTRACTIVE

Magnets pull magnetic materials such as iron and steel toward them. This pull is called attraction. The stronger the magnet, the stronger its attractive force. Modern household items have many ingenious uses for magnetic attraction. Did you know that a magnet is often used on a refrigerator door to hold it firmly closed?

MAKE A FUNNY FACE

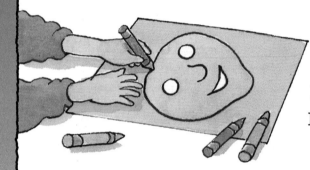

1 Draw the shape of a face on a sheet of thin cardboard. Make the eyes, nose and mouth especially large. Don't draw in any hair or eyebrows.

2 Ask an adult to make some iron filings for you by filing down a nail. Pour the iron filings onto the cardboard in a few places.

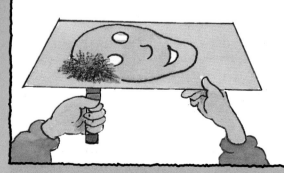

3 Hold the cardboard with one hand and bring a magnet under it with the other. The magnet will attract the iron filings through the cardboard.

3 Gently tap the cardboard. Examine the pattern made by the filings. You will see that the filings form lines. These show you where the magnetic field lies.

WHY IT WORKS

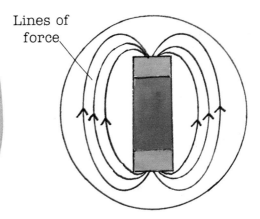

Lines of force

Each filing is attracted to the magnet along invisible lines of force. These make up the magnetic field. The filings are small enough to show the direction in which the field is pulling.

FURTHER IDEAS

Try the experiment again using a horseshoe or ring-shaped magnet. What kind of pattern do the iron filings make?

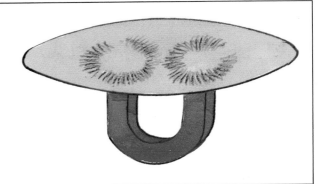

NORTH AND SOUTH

For centuries travelers have found their way with the help of a compass. Inside a compass is a small magnetic pointer. It spins around but always comes to rest pointing north. From knowing where north is, it is easy to locate south, west and east.

MAKE A COMPASS

1 Stroke a nail with one end of a magnet. Make sure you pass the magnet in one direction only. Stroke the nail about 20 times.

2 Ask an adult to slice a piece of cork. Now tape the magnetized nail to it.

GET AN ADULT TO HELP YOU WITH THIS

3 Float the cork in a basin of water. Leave until the nail stops moving. Make sure there are no magnetic objects nearby.

WHY IT WORKS

4 The nail will point either north or south. Find out which way it is pointing, then make labels for north, south, west and east.

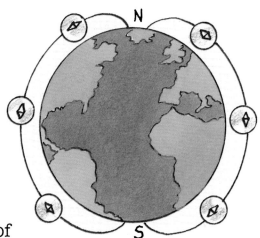

The north pole of a magnet seeks out the north pole of the Earth. It is as if the Earth contained a gigantic magnet. The north pole of the Earth attracts any smaller magnets so that when allowed to, they always point north.

FURTHER IDEAS

Tie a piece of thread around the middle of a bar magnet. Suspend the magnet from the back of a chair. Watch to see if the poles point north-south. What happens when other magnetic objects are close to the magnet?

HIDDEN MAGNETS

You may be surprised how important magnets are in modern machines. Computers use magnetic floppy disks to store huge amounts of information. Tape recorders and video recorders use magnetic tape to store film, sound, and music. These are hidden magnets.

THE AMAZING MAGIC FINGER

1 Magnetize a steel nail by stroking it in one direction with a magnet. Stroke at least 20 times (see page 184).

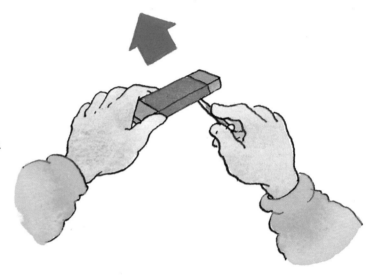

2 Carefully tape the nail to your index finger. Make sure the point cannot hurt anyone.

3 Find an old glove that fits your hand snugly. Put it on to hide the magnetized nail.

4 Bring your magic finger close to a compass needle. Amaze your friends by making the compass needle swing around.

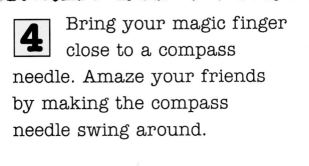

Unmagnetized nail

Magnetized nail

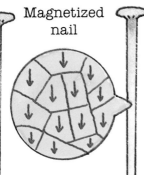

The metal in the nail is made up of millions of tiny crystals. Each can behave like a tiny magnet but they point in different directions. Stroking the nail with a magnet makes each crystal point the same way. This causes the nail to become magnetized.

FURTHER IDEAS
Use your magic finger for other magic tricks. Impress your friends by balancing a pin or nail right on the end of your finger.

ELECTROMAGNETISM

An electromagnet is a coil of wire around an iron core. You may have seen a crane that has an electromagnet instead of a hook to carry things. Powerful electromagnets can lift heavy iron loads, even whole cars. The load is dropped by switching off the electromagnet.

MAKE AN ELECTROMAGNET

1 Take a cardboard box. Make holes in the center of three sides. Cut two strips of cardboard. Make three holes in each strip (see right).

Holes

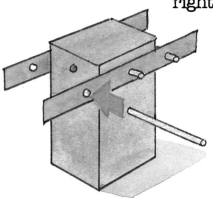

2 Push three pieces of stick through the holes in the strips of cardboard and the box (left). This is your crane arm.

3 Color some smaller boxes to make them look like cars or an iron bar. Glue a steel washer to the top of each one.

4 Take 2 to 3 feet of plastic-coated wire and coil around an iron nail. Connect the wire to the terminals of a battery.

5 Hide the battery in the box. Push the nail and wire through the hole in the front of the crane. Use the electromagnet to pick up paper clips. Switch it off by removing the wire from the battery.

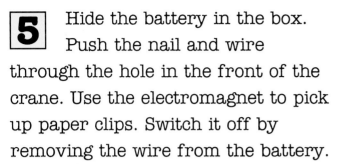

Nail becomes magnetized

Electricity flowing along a wire has a magnetic field around it. The field is made stronger by coiling the wire. The nail inside the coils becomes magnetized by the field. Each part of the iron nail lines up facing the same direction, running from north to south.

FURTHER IDEAS
Experiment with your electromagnet by changing the number of coils around the nail. What happens when there are fewer coils? What happens when there are more?

CONTENTS

CHAPTER *Eight*

HEARING SOUNDS

WHAT IS A SOUND?

All sounds are made by something moving. Gently rest your fingertips on your throat as you talk. You can feel your throat vibrating. Vocal cords in your throat move as you speak and make the air in your throat and mouth vibrate. The vibrating air makes sounds.

MAKE A BANGER

1 Take a square sheet of paper and decorate it. Fold it in half diagonally to make a triangle (see right).

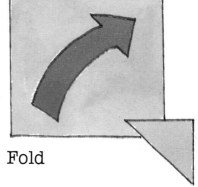

Fold

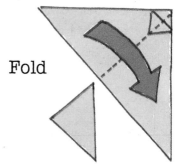

Fold

2 Fold the top right-hand corner downward.

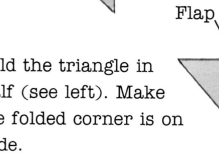

Flap

3 Fold the triangle in half (see left). Make sure the folded corner is on the inside.

4 Make a crease down the middle but do not fold in half.

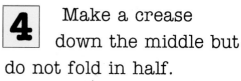

Crease

5 From the open end of the triangle fold the top layer of paper over along the crease. Flip the triangle over and repeat.

Fold

6 Grasp the three pointed ends of the triangle together. Flick your wrist down to make the banger work.

WHY IT WORKS

Flicking your wrist makes the folded paper jump out of place. The paper pushes hard against the air. The pushed air reaches your ears as a "bang."

Air

FURTHER IDEAS
Try making different-sized bangers. Follow the same steps with the largest square of paper you can find. Repeat with the smallest square of paper.

MAKING A SOUND

Sounds travel through the air to reach our ears. On a very windy day, the wind can blow sounds away from you so it is difficult to hear a conversation. If sounds have traveled a long way then they lose some loudness. Sounds made close to us seem louder.

MAKE A BULL ROARER

1 You will need a long cardboard tube, scissors, a ruler, about 19 inches of clothing elastic and 3 to 6 feet of string.

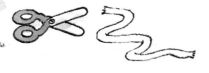

2 Loop the elastic through the tube. Knot the two ends together firmly.

3 Knot one end of the string around the elastic at the opening of the tube.

4 Take the other end of the string in your hand and swing the bull roarer around. Listen to the sound it makes.

WHY IT WORKS

As the tube spins around, air enters and pushes the elastic rapidly backward and forward. Air leaving the tube carries the sounds made from these movements.

Air carrying sound out

Air in

FURTHER IDEAS
Experiment with the bull roarer by using a shorter length of string. If you have room, try a longer length. Listen carefully. How does the difference in length affect the sound?

GOOD VIBRATIONS

Pleasant sounds can come from musical instruments. All musical instruments have parts that move to make vibrations. Vibrations are caused by something moving back and forth very quickly and smoothly. A drum has a head that vibrates when it is hit with a stick. The harder you hit the drum, the bigger the vibrations and the louder the sound.

MAKE A DRUM

1 You will need a large, empty tin can and a clean plastic bag. Carefully cut a circle out of the plastic bag. Make sure it is larger than the can.

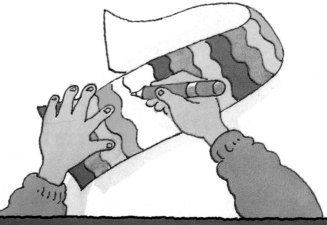

2 Stretch the circle of plastic as tightly as you can over the rim of the empty can. Hold it in place with tape.

3 Cut a strip of paper the same width as the can and long enough to go all the way around it. Color it brightly and tape into place.

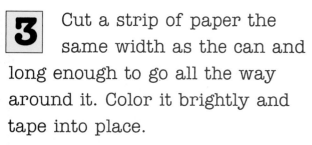

4 Make a pair of drumsticks with wooden dowels. Wrap the tips in cotton and cover with a piece of stocking. Tie into place with string.

5 Test your drum. Hit the drumhead gently in different places and compare the sounds of different vibrations. Try to play a rhythm.

WHY IT WORKS

When you hit the drumhead it vibrates. The air inside the drum vibrates too. These vibrations of air are called sound waves.

FURTHER IDEAS
The movement of the vibrating drumhead is too small to see. Try placing some dried peas on the drum to show the effect of the vibrations.

THE SOUND DRUM

We cannot see sounds but we can see their effects. Sounds travel through the air just like waves in the sea. If the waves are strong enough they can move things in their path. The human ear has an eardrum that moves when hit by sound waves entering the ear.

MAKE A SOUND DRUM

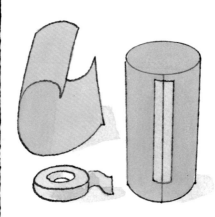

1 Roll a strong sheet of cardboard into a tube. Make sure the cardboard overlaps so that it can be taped together.

2 Cut a circle larger than the end of your tube out of a clean plastic bag. Tape it as tightly as possible over one end of the tube.

3 Cut a cardboard circle the same size. Cut a hole in the middle of it. Tape the circle over the other end of the tube.

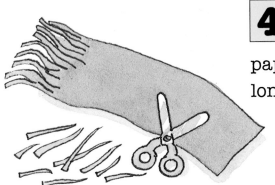

4 Make a target out of a long strip of tissue paper. Cut one end into a long fringe.

5 Point the hole in the bottom of your sound drum toward your target. Tap the plastic drumhead. What happens to your target?

WHY IT WORKS

Tapping the drumhead pushes sound waves through the hole in the bottom of the drum. It also forces rings of air out through the hole, which moves the paper fringe.

FURTHER IDEAS
You need a partner to help you. Take turns to hit the sound drum and hold the target. What is the farthest distance you can hit the target from?

LISTEN CLOSELY

If you are ill a doctor may use a stethoscope to listen to your heart or lungs. You may have a problem breathing or your heart may not be making the sounds it is supposed to. These sounds are normally too quiet to hear. A stethoscope magnifies them so they can be heard.

MAKE A STETHOSCOPE

1 Cut out two large paper circles. Color them brightly. Make a long cardboard tube. Decorate this too.

2 Cut a hole in the center of each circle the same size as the tube end. Cut from the hole to the edge of the circle. Tape the edges to form two cones.

3 Tape one cone shape over each end of the tube. Make the fit as snug as possible.

sound in

4 Now try out your stethoscope. Put your ear to one cone and place the other on a friend's chest.

WHY IT WORKS

As sound waves spread out they become smaller and harder to hear. The first cone stops them from spreading by collecting them together. They move along the tube and out through the second cone into your ear.

FURTHER IDEAS
Use your stethoscope to compare the sound of your heartbeat with your friend's heartbeat. Try to think of other quiet sounds to listen to, such as a friend whispering or a ticking watch.

BOUNCING SOUNDS

Bats have very poor eyesight yet can fly around safely in complete darkness. They can avoid hitting obstacles by bouncing squeaky sounds off them. Bouncing sounds are called echoes. You can hear echoes in places such as large halls or gyms when sounds bounce off the walls.

BOUNCE AN ECHO

2 One cone is a hearing aid, the other a megaphone to magnify sounds.

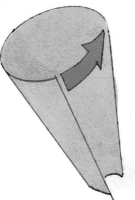

1 Cut the shape shown here out of cardboard. Overlap the edges and tape to make a cone. Repeat so you have two large cones.

3 Cut out two strips of cardboard. Tape them along the sides of your hearing aid and megaphone to make handles.

WHY IT WORKS

When a sound wave hits something it can either be absorbed or bounce off. Smooth, flat surfaces bounce sounds best. The sound of your voice bounces off the mirror just as light would.

Hearing aid

Megaphone

FURTHER IDEAS
Try to bounce sounds off other surfaces. You could compare a cork tile, an egg carton and a wooden block. Which reflects sound waves best?

4 Talk into the megaphone aimed at a mirror or tin tray. A friend can hear your voice echo with the hearing aid.

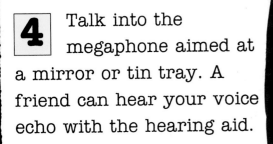

KEEPING SOUNDS IN

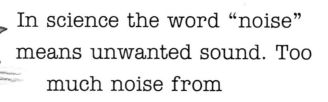

In science the word "noise" means unwanted sound. Too much noise from airplanes or discos is bad for your health. It can keep you from sleeping and even damage your eardrums. A radio studio is soundproofed. Noise is kept out so that it cannot be heard when programs are broadcast.

MAKE A SOUNDPROOF BOX

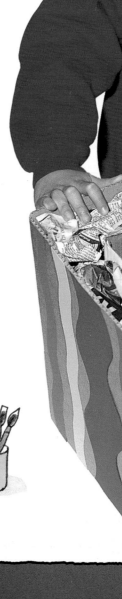

1 You need a large cardboard box and a shoe box, both with lids. The shoe box must easily fit inside the cardboard box.

2 Decorate the outside of the cardboard box. Use brightly colored paints. When dry, place the shoe box inside the larger box.

3 Pack the space between the boxes with crumpled newspapers. Add a little paper to the inner box.

WHY IT WORKS

Sound waves from the alarm cannot escape from the soundproof box. Most sound waves are absorbed by the cardboard and the newspaper. You may hear just a few sound waves leaking out.

4 Set off an alarm clock and place it in the inner box. Close the lids of both boxes. What can you hear?

FURTHER IDEAS
Try to improve the soundproofing by replacing the newspaper with egg cartons or sawdust. Make it a fair test by using the same alarm clock each time.

VIBRATING AIR

An orchestra has percussion, wind, and stringed instruments. Wind instruments include flutes, clarinets, and recorders. They are all made out of a tube. When the instrument is played, air inside the tube vibrates and makes sound. Instruments make different sounds because they vary in shape and size.

MAKE A CLARINET

1 Use stiff cardboard to make a cone as shown on page 202. Make sure the small opening at the top is less than half an inch across.

2 Use sharp scissors to cut a "V" shape from the end of a drinking straw.

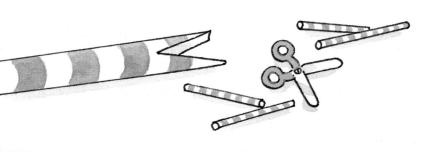

3 Hold the cut end of the straw between your thumb and finger. Pinch the ends together to flatten them.

4 Cut off the pinched end of the straw. Push it into the small opening of the cone.

Sound out

5 Try out your clarinet. Put the mouthpiece inside your mouth and blow into the cone. Feel it vibrate as you play a note.

Mouthpiece

FURTHER IDEAS
Make more clarinets using cones of different sizes. Each needs a straw mouthpiece as before. Compare the kinds of notes you get with long and short clarinets.
Using your different-sized clarinets can you and your friends play a tune?

WHY IT WORKS

Blowing through the sharp edges of the straw makes them vibrate. The vibrating straw makes all the air in the cone vibrate and causes sound. We hear these sound waves escaping from the cone.

DIFFERENT PITCHES

Most musical instruments can make a wide range of notes – from low or deep notes that you may be able to feel, to high notes you can only just hear.

Notes differ in pitch. Pitch measures how high or low a note is.

MAKE A XYLOPHONE

GET AN ADULT TO DO THIS FOR YOU

1 Cut five circles in the lid of a box, big enough for glass bottles to fit.

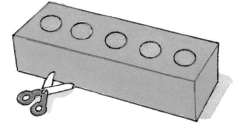

2 Check that the bottles fit snugly into place. Tape a sheet of cardboard to stand up behind them.

3 Fill each bottle with a different amount of water. Line them up with the fullest at one end and the emptiest at the other.

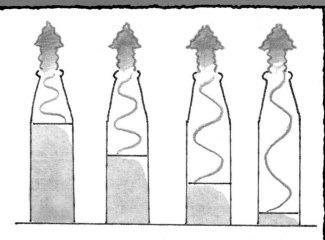

WHY IT WORKS

Above the water level each bottle contains a tube of air. Hitting the bottles makes the air vibrate. Longer tubes of air (emptier bottles) vibrate more slowly. Slower vibrations make deeper (lower-pitched) sounds.

4 Tap the neck of each bottle with a stick or wooden spoon. Note the different sounds they make. See if you can play a tune.

FURTHER IDEAS
You can make the air in the bottles vibrate another way. Rest your lip on the bottle top and blow.

VIBRATING STRINGS

Stringed instruments include violins, harps, and guitars. Musicians hit or pluck the strings to make them vibrate. Each string is of a different thickness and tautness so each makes a different note. Musicians also change the notes by altering the length of the vibrating string.

MAKE A GUITAR

1 Wash out a large margarine tub. Cut an oval-shaped hole in the lid with a sharp knife or pair of scissors.

GET AN ADULT TO DO THIS FOR YOU

2 Use brightly colored magic markers to decorate the outside of the tub and lid.

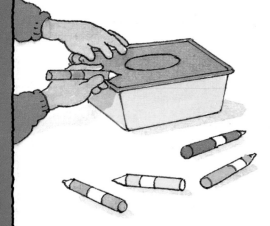

3 Wrap six rubber bands of differing thickness lengthwise around the tub. Leave a space between each rubber band.

4 Pluck each rubber band with your finger. Compare the sounds made by plucking the ends or middle of each rubber band.

Slower vibrations - lower notes

Faster vibrations - higher notes

WHY IT WORKS

A vibrating rubber band makes the air in the tub vibrate. This makes sound waves which escape through the hole in the lid. Thin rubber bands vibrate much faster than thicker ones. Faster vibrations make higher notes.

FURTHER IDEAS

Place a pencil between the rubber bands and the lid of the tub. This alters the length of the rubber bands and changes the notes they make. Experiment with the pencil in different places along the tub.

TUNING UP

Musicians have to "tune" their instruments. For a stringed instrument this means adjusting each string to just the right tautness to play the correct note. If a string is too slack, it cannot vibrate properly. If it is too taut then the string might snap.

MAKE A SONOMETER

1 You will need a large sheet of thick cardboard. Divide it roughly into thirds. Decorate one side with colored magic markers.

GET AN ADULT TO DO THIS FOR YOU

2 Very carefully use a sharp knife to cut a notch into the sides of two wooden pencils.

3 Find a piece of nylon fishing line about three feet long. Firmly push a thumbtack into one end of the cardboard. Tie one end of the thread to the thumbtack.

4 Tape the notched pencils into place. Lay the fishing line in the two notches. Tie the other end of the line around a plastic cup weighted down with marbles or stones.

5 Hang the cup over the edge of a table. Pluck the fishing line. Listen to the sound change when you add marbles to the cup.

WHY IT WORKS

Hanging more weight from the fishing line pulls it tighter. This causes it to vibrate faster. The faster the vibrations are, the higher the note sounds to us.

FURTHER IDEAS
Change the length of fishing line you pluck by moving the pencils closer together or farther apart. Try to predict the length of line and weight to attach to get the highest and lowest possible notes.

FARAWAY SOUNDS

Listening to the ground is an excellent way of listening to faraway sounds. This is because sounds travel faster through the ground than through air. You may have seen a bandit in a cowboy film put his ear to a railway track. Today railway workers use this method to listen for trains. They hear sound trapped in the rails before they see the train.

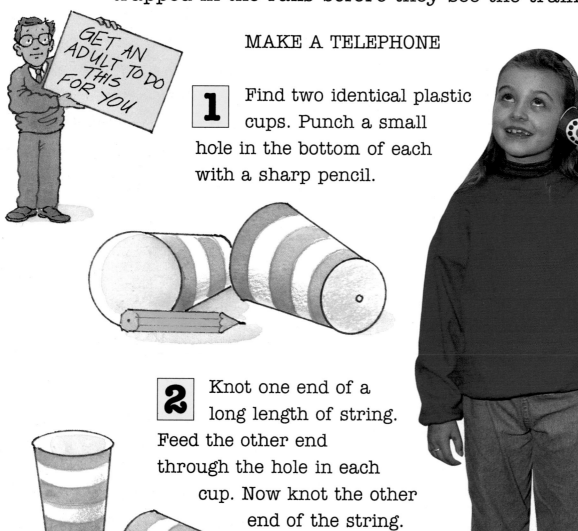

GET AN ADULT TO DO THIS FOR YOU

MAKE A TELEPHONE

1 Find two identical plastic cups. Punch a small hole in the bottom of each with a sharp pencil.

2 Knot one end of a long length of string. Feed the other end through the hole in each cup. Now knot the other end of the string.

3 Check that the string cannot be easily tugged out of place. Decorate each telephone cup. Use brightly colored magic markers.

WHY IT WORKS

The sounds you make travel along the string as tiny vibrations (you can just feel them if you touch the string). They travel through the plastic cup and the air to reach your ear.

4 With a partner, each take a cup and pull the string taut. Put your cup to your ear. Ask your partner to talk into his or hers. Try to have a conversation.

FURTHER IDEAS
Tie a fork and spoon to a piece of string. Hold the other end of the string to one ear; cover up your other ear. You can "feel" the sound of the jangling utensils. The sounds travel up through the string.

GLOSSARY

Acid
A liquid that turns blue litmus (an indicator) red. Many occur naturally; hydrochloric acid is found in the stomach and helps food digestion.

Alkali
A liquid that turns red litmus (an indicator) blue.

Arch
A shape, roughly semicircular, that is capable of supporting a great deal of weight.

Atom
The smallest complete particle that everything is made up of. Atoms are made up of smaller particles called electrons, protons, and neutrons.

Attract
To pull something toward you.

Ballast
Extra weight carried by vessels. It can be solid or liquid. Ballast helps keep a boat stable. When pumped out, it helps increase buoyancy.

Buoyancy
The ability of a substance to float. Buoyancy depends on the density of the object.

Charge
Electric charge can be either positive or negative. Inside atoms, electrons carry a negative charge and protons carry a positive charge.

Chlorophyll
Chemical pigment that gives green plants their color. It traps the energy contained in sunlight needed for photosynthesis.

Circuit
A complete path around which an electric current can flow.

Compass
An instrument with a magnetized pointer. The pointer always points north because it always lines itself with the Earth's magnetic field.

Compress
To squeeze together into less space.

Conductor
Any material that allows electricity to pass through it.

Convection currents
Circular movements in fluids caused by warm substances rising, cooling, and then falling again.

Crystal
A solid body in which the atoms are arranged in a rigid structure.

Current
A flow of negative charge (electrons) around a circuit.

Density
The weight or heaviness of an object when it takes up a given amount of space.

Drag
The resistance of air or water. A force that holds back moving objects.

Eardrum
A sheet of skin inside your ear. Sounds in the air set it vibrating just like a drumhead. Messages to the brain tell you what the sound is like.

Echo
The reflection or bouncing back of a sound from a surface.

Elastic
An elastic object will recover its original shape after being molded.

Electric motor
A machine that turns electricity into movement by using a magnet.

Electrolyte
A liquid in which a chemical reaction takes place when an electric current flows through it.

Electromagnet
A coil of wire with an iron bar inside it. It becomes a magnet only when electricity is flowing through the coil.

Electroscope
A device used by scientists to measure how much static electricity is contained in an object.

Energy
When a force moves an object, energy is passed to the object (where it may be saved). Heat, light and power are familiar forms of energy.

Filter
A process to purify substances by removing impurities.

Force
A push, pull, or twist that makes an object move or change direction. For example, throwing a ball is exerting force on the ball which makes it move.

Freeze
When a substance turns from a liquid into a solid as its temperature drops.

Frequency
The number of sound vibrations that happen in one second.

Friction
A force that occurs when two surfaces rub against each other. It always slows movement, and brings motion to a stop if no other force is applied to overcome it.

Gravity
The pulling force of the Earth that makes things fall, and gives things weight.

Grip
The action of a surface on another as a result of friction.

Gyroscope
A spinning top that stays upright even if its surroundings are moved.

Hydraulics
The use of liquids, particularly water, in engineering. Hydraulic systems are used for transmitting energy.

GLOSSARY

Hydrometer
Instrument used to measure the density of a liquid by how deeply it sinks into the liquid.

Image
The "picture" of an object usually formed by a lens or photograph.

Indicator
Shows the chemical conditions of a substance by changing color. Litmus turns red for acids, green for alkalis and blue for neutrals.

Induced magnetism
Magnetism caused in magnetic material such as iron or steel, when a permanent magnet is brought very close.

Insulator
Any material that does not let electricity pass through it.

Jet
A fast-moving flow of water or air forced through a small outlet.

Light ray
A very narrow beam of light.

Line of force
A line that shows the magnetic effect around a magnet.

Litmus
An indicator that turns red in acids and blue in alkalis.

Lodestone
A type of rock which is a natural magnet.

Magnetic field
The area around a magnet where the magnetic force works.

Magnetic material
Material that can be made into or attracted to a magnet.

Magnetic pole
Place on a magnet where the magnetic force is strongest. Poles can be north and south.

Magnetize
To turn a magnetic material into a magnet.

Melt
To change from a solid to a liquid when the temperature rises.

Microbe
A microscopic living organism.

Möbius strip
A surface that has only one side. It is made by joining the two ends of a strip that has been twisted around once.

Molecule
Smallest particle of a substance that still has the substance's properties. A molecule may contain several atoms.

Note
A steady sound or tone of the same pitch or frequency.

Oxidize
To combine a substance with oxygen.

Particle
A tiny piece of a substance.

Percussion
Musical instruments played by hitting two things together; for example, a drum and drumstick.

Permanent magnet
A magnet that keeps its magnetism unless it is dropped, knocked, or gets too hot.

Photosynthesis
A chemical process where light energy trapped by chlorophyll combines with water and air to help make a plant grow.

Pigment
The substance added to paints and dyes to give them their color.

Pitch
The highness or lowness of a sound. Pitch depends on the frequency of the vibration causing the sound.

Plastic
When a body can be shaped into a new form, it is said to be plastic. Its properties allow it to be molded and then retain its new shape.

Port
The left side of a boat or ship as you look forward.

Power
The rate at which energy is changed from one form to another. The power of moving car engines is measured in brake horsepower (bhp).

Pressure
The force which presses down on a given area.

Primary color
There are three primary colors of paints and dyes, from which all other colors are made: red, yellow, and blue.

Prism
A transparent wedge, usually of glass, used to split white light into the colors of the rainbow.

Propeller
A rotating object with spiral arms used to drive a boat or other vessel forward.

Pulley
A system of wheels and rope that allows heavy loads to be lifted more easily.

Reflect
When light or sound is bounced back from a surface.

Repel
To push apart. Two south or two north poles repel each other.

Resistance
The ability that a material has to stop or resist the flow of electric current through it.

GLOSSARY

Rigid
When an object is stiff and inflexible, it is said to be rigid. Its structure will not allow it to be bent or formed into any other shape.

Rudder
A flat steering object found under the stern of and underneath a boat.

Saturated
When a substance has been filled to its fullest possible extent.

Shadow
Place of darkness created by an object blocking light.

Sound wave
A regular pattern of vibrations that move through the air or other materials.

Starboard
The right side of a boat or ship as you look forward.

Stethoscope
Instrument used by doctors to hear sounds within the body which are normally too quiet to hear.

Structure
The arrangement of parts to form an entire object.

Temperature
The level of heat that a body has. It is measured in degrees of Celsius, Fahrenheit, and Kelvin.

Terminal
The part of a battery to which wires can be attached.

Tessellation
The ability of shapes to fit together neatly and cover an area without overlapping or leaving any spaces.

Thermal
An ascending current of warm air.

Tiller
The handle used to turn a rudder.

Vibration
A rapid backward and forward movement.

Vocal cord
Flaps of elastic tissue in the human throat which vibrate as air from the lungs is pushed over them, producing the sounds of the human voice.

Volume
The amount of space something takes up.

Weaving
To form a fabric by interlacing fibers. The weft threads are woven through the warp threads, to create the finished cloth.

Woodwind
Wind instruments made from wood or sometimes silver; for example, a clarinet or a flute.

INDEX

INDEX

INDEX

4 Arrange the iron filings with the magnet to give your face hair, eyebrows and a beard. Move the magnet away from your funny face.

WHY IT WORKS

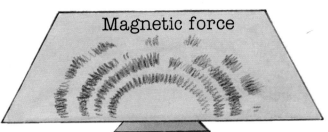

Magnetic force

Magnet

The magnetic force pulls on each tiny piece of iron filing. As you move the magnet under the cardboard the filings are dragged along. When you move the magnet away the iron filings stay in place.

FURTHER IDEAS

Test the strength of your magnet. Use it to move a pin through one page of a book, then through two pages, then three pages and so on until the pages block the magnetic force.

INVISIBLE PATTERNS

Magnetic objects close to a magnet are attracted to it. There is a "field" (space) around the magnet where the magnetic force works. We cannot see this field but can feel its pull on objects. Scientists have discovered that birds use the Earth's magnetic field to guide them on long journeys.

SEE A MAGNETIC FIELD

1 Use a pair of compasses to draw a circle on a sheet of cardboard. Cut out the circle and tape a bar magnet in the center.

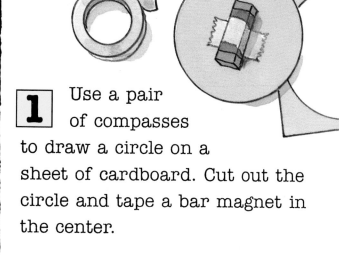

2 Turn the cardboard over so the magnet is underneath. Evenly sprinkle some iron filings (see page 180) over the surface of the cardboard.